MW01630536

# The Potts Factor's Return

# The Potts Factor's Return

*by*

**Stanley Potts**

Other Books by Stanley Potts:

**The Potts' Factor Versus Murphy's Law**

**Look Down on the Stars**


**Stanley Potts**
4 Redside Way
Shoup, Idaho 83469
Website: thepottsfactor.com
Email: thepottsfactor@salmoninternet.com
(208) 394-2135

ISBN (Softbound): 1-56684-682-X
978-1-56684-682-0

(Hardbound): 1-56684-681-1
978-1-56684-681-3

Library of Congress Catalogue Card Number 2006934198

# Introduction

Well, this is the third attempt to report some more of the happenings of my life so I guess they will be a trilogy.

My first two books have been somewhat successful. (I sold one each to most of my relations and both of my friends!) With more relations or more friends they would be really successful!

People have told me "Man you write like a combination of Pat McManus, Dave Barry and Baxter Black!" I read some of their stuff and "Sure enough! We all write in English!" (My apologies to all three for any comparison beyond writing in English.)

Other people have said, "You will never be accused of being a writer – But you tell a hell of a good story in print!"

Whatever the case may be – here are more of my stories in print. All true to the best of my ability to report. The stories about others – are the best from my memory and theirs. The stories are not sequential; any one of them will lull you to sleep as well as the rest.

# Acknowledgements

I would like to thank a couple of the legends of Idaho mountain flying that helped me with stories, maps, newspaper and magazine clippings, etc. That helped me put the finishing touches on the Boise Airstrip – Bill Woods Story.

Dick Waite of Hagerman, Idaho and Harold Dougal of Boise, Idaho, both with ten times or more of my flying time that we were all privileged to enjoy in the Idaho backcountry. Captain Harold Dougal allowed me to use a few captions from his book "Idaho Mountain Pilot."

**DICK WAITE'S DAUGHTERS, MARILYN AND BZ, PROUDLY WATCH THEIR FATHER RECEIVE THE FEDERAL AVIATION ADMINISTRATION WRIGHT BROTHERS MASTER PILOT AWARD AFTER 60+ YEARS OF FLYING. ONLY THE 38th RECIPIENT SINCE ORVILLE COAXED THE FIRST PLANE INTO THE AIR.**

The Arco Advertiser for use of portions of their articles and pictures I used on Val Goodman's life in three different centuries.

To Val's son Bob Stanford Evans, of Hemet, California, for much more information and much needed pictures to help with the story.

To my wife of fifty-two years for putting up with me and my rattling around the house, at all hours of the night looking for pictures and information for the book. Thanks, Joy!

And lastly to Bobbie Balis of Colson Creek and Bellevue, Idaho for typing my scribbles and putting them in readable form and on a disk for the printers.  Many, many, thanks Bobbie!

# Dedication

I would like to dedicate this book to my dad Verl Potts. He was born July 12, 1905 and passed away February 6, 1993.

He taught me a variety of important things. Two of the most valuable are honesty and punctuality. Don't fudge on the truth and if you are late for an appointment you better have a damn good reason.

Hard work is necessary in the lifestyle we lived, and there is a strong mental satisfaction that stems from a job well done. Consider yourself lucky to be able to work hard and enjoy it. Remember a lot of people either can't or won't and therefore miss out on that satisfaction.

How to survive out in the mountains – lots of important things, but the absolute most important is, being able to start a fire with the simple ingredients that you carry with you and on your person at all times.

A waterproof match container and a couple sticks of pitch wood would have saved untold lives, frozen feet and limbs, not to mention the enjoyable difference between a warm crackling fire and the silence of the cold.

Not being able to build a fire may have cost Rulon Gardiner his second Olympic Gold Medal. Besides having a horribly long cold night and losing one of his toes, he could have lost his life as well.

Dad was only 5'8" and about 165 pounds but he kept in good physical condition all of his life. He would crawl out of bed and do twenty or thirty pushups before he got dressed.

He could outrun me at all distances all of his life. When I was in high school and on the track team I thought I could run a little. Hah! He'd beat me at 100yds, 440yds or one mile. We'd run before breakfast and on the mile run he would be washed up and starting breakfast when I puffed my way home. I kept thinking when he was 80 that if he lived to be 90 I might finally be able to outrun him. Alas, it was not to be.

He was a good boxer and a better street fighter as lots of guys found out the hard way. He tried to teach me but I kept leading with my nose!

We partnered on several ventures, but because of two strong personalities (as in a hard headed pair), we had far better luck if each of us did an individual portion of the job.

**Thanks Dad, for the teachings and the memories!**

# Table of Contents

# Foreword

Stanley Potts is so comfortable within himself that he can be sitting all alone at the top of a vast mountain range, flying up in the clouds in his airplane. Stan can be with a small group exchanging hunting stories by a campfire, or one on one with a neighbor having coffee in their living room. Stan is content to have the whole family around when they come to visit or sitting on the deck with wife Joy at home. Put him on an animal in his beloved wilderness and he would probably be happier and more content than in a luxury car.

In reading his first book, "The Potts' Factor Versus Murphy's Law," you get a sense of the adventure, fearlessness, and BAD LUCK that made up most of Stan's' life. He handled all that life dished out and gave back the same. When reading the second book, "Look Down On The Stars," the people, places, trips and adventures abound. His love of family and friends shine through in his writing.

Stan is a great story teller and he is just the person to be telling stories because he has lived a story tellers' life. Most people can tell a good story, but only one that they have heard, Stan tells a good story he has "Lived!"

I offered to help Stan, in his third book endeavor, by typing his story from the many hand written pages he gave me. Stan has no idea how hard it was for me to type these wonderful stories. I would get so busy reading ahead of my typing that I would have to correct myself over and over again.

His stories make you laugh at his missteps, they capture your imagination, make you cry over his losses and wonder at the sights he has seen.

I would gladly read (I mean type), any book Stan writes in the future. I know he will have many more stories to come, he is just to busy (not lucky enough), to not have more adventures happening in his life. We all look forward to more!!!

Bobbie Balis
Bellevue, Idaho
March 23, 2006

# Chapter 1

## To Sight in a Rifle with One Shell

Won time, many daze ago, eye was going to sea if eye could right a story about the write weigh two site in a rifle with only won cartridge.

I realized about then that I should have concentrated somewhat more on the rudiments of the language known as English. I think this guy "English" that invented it could have made it a little simpler as there are lengthy groups of words that sound exactly the same with very different spellings and meanings.

Basically, attention to my English teachers attempts to teach me something, instead of studying the maximum distance and trajectory of a large spit wad, may have helped somewhat. I remember, vaguely I might add, some phrases and rules, "Eye befour e except after sea." It never made any cents then either.

"Prepositional phrase," (not to be confused with), "Propositional phrase," of which I have obtained some familiarity with later on.

"Sentence," a group of words connected together in random order to convey meaning to a story. One sentence should usually be no longer than a page or two.

"Paragraph," a couple or three connected sentences which can usually make up a chapter of moderate length. (Long chapters can occasionally demand four sentences with a chapter of thirty pages or more, making use of five or GASP! even six sentences.)

I have seriously attempted to master this portion of the English language and, I might add, feel I have succeeded quite successfully!

"Comma," a very valuable little squiggly mark added wherever you can't think of anything else to write. This gives you a few moments up to a few days to collect and organize your thought processes. You can then carry on right behind the little squiggly thing without the necessity of a period.

"Period," little dot type thing used very sparingly and then only after all thought processes have completely shut down.

"Quotation Marks," are double little squiggly things thrown randomly at a group of words. They are purported to convey the impression that you have some clue to their value.

"Indentation," is a method of moving a few words out of the straight line of your lengthy sentences. It appears to be of more value on the left side of the page and assists the reader (assuming there is one), in more easily finding his or her place after their nap from the boredom of your story.

As near as I can tell it should be used after a period rather than a comma, although I favor an occasional indentation after a comma in an attempt to keep the possible reader alert.

"Hyphen", no idea what it is for but I like to put the little horizontal flat mark between a couple words every now and then just to give the impression that I do.

"Parentheses", a couple of curved lines enclosing several words and inserted randomly to give the impression that they may be of some importance.

With this explanation of my entire grasp of the English language I will now go on with the method of sighting in a rifle with one shell.

This method probably wouldn't allow you to win the one thousand yard match at Camp Perry but it would allow you to shoot within a few inch circle at one hundred yards.

This method is used when the gun bearer is short of bullets, low on ammo, or maybe only has two shells left (known as very short of ammo)!

1) You will need some type of large target – preferably a couple of feet in diameter.
2) It must be something that will not move after the bullet hits it and must clearly show the bullet hole. Draw a good aim point on the target.
3) Get back about twenty yards or so.
4) Bore sight the rifle as closely as possible.
5) Place the rifle solidly over a rest. (Log, rock, table or rolled up sleeping bag will work).
6) Hold crosshairs steadily on aim point and shoot your bullet.
7) Find the bullet hole and once again hold crosshairs or sight on aim point and adjust sight adjustments to the bullet hole. The gun must not move – only the adjustment of the sight.
8) Rifle barrel and sights are now on the same spot and will enable the gun to place your bullet in a few inch circle at moderate ranges.

# Chapter 2

## The Lucky Sticks

The cover of this book has a couple of interesting pictures on it.

The first one is an airplane sitting out in the middle of the Salmon River; next to it is a photo of three non-descript wooden sticks.

I will attempt to summarize the possible connection for you to contemplate in the next couple of stories, plus the possible links to other events chronicled in past books.

My wife Joy and I were on a desert sheep hunt in Nevada many years ago. We were splitting up and hiking in different directions each day in an attempt to find a good desert ram for Joy to hunt.

One afternoon I was hiking along the floor of the desert back toward our Jeep station wagon when I spotted an interesting cave up on the hillside a hundred yards or so. There were desert sheep tracks all around the entrance so I decided to look around in the cave.

When I arrived at the cave entrance I could see it was fire blackened so assumed it had been used by primitive people, probably Indians.

The cave entrance was barely four feet high with the interior ceiling going up to six or seven feet. It was not too large a cave – maybe ten or twelve feet across. There were sheep tracks and droppings on the floor of the cave and it was nice and cool so I was pretty sure the sheep used it for shade during hot summer days.

It was quite dark inside so I turned on my flashlight to look around for petroglyphs, spear points, arrowheads etc.

On the ceiling of the cave wedged in a crack in the rocks was what appeared to be a small bundle of sticks. My initial reaction was that it had been placed there as a supply of dry wood for fire starter. I carefully removed the sticks from the rock fissure and went outside into the sunlight.

The stick bundle consisted of three sticks of creosote bush, each about one half inch in diameter and of three different lengths of approximately one foot, two feet and three feet. A sharp object like a knife of some sort had cut some of the ends.

The stick bundle was tied together with fibers from what appeared to have been stripped from a nearby Joshua tree. They had been wrapped about three times and listen to this; the ends were tied with square knots! I have tried to teach some of my guides to tie square knots for years (unsuccessfully, I might add). And here are square knots tied by a primitive people.

There were lots of chips from different colored rocks where the cave dwellers had fabricated some of their tools, probably axes, spear points and arrowheads. I tied the stick bundle to my pack frame and carried it back to show Joy.

Later we were in a museum of the Southwest and in one of the glass display cases were a couple of nearly identical stick packages. We asked the curator what they were and he told us that from what could be determined from Indian legends, the stick bundles were a sort of good luck charm – to protect the owner's home, cave, hogan, lodge or whatever from danger.

Who knows? But I am not planning on using mine for kindling to start a fire anytime in the near future!

Those of you who have read my other books, **"The Potts Factor Versus Murphy's Law"** and **"Look Down On The Stars"** and are able to get through this one will probably understand why! The old saying, "Don't rock the apple cart" seems to come into play here.

The bundle of sticks weren't a good luck charm for Joy's desert ram though. We looked at forty-seven desert rams but succeeded in coming home without a ram. She tried a long shot at a giant ram but her guide "Me", had her hold the aim point too high and the ram ran off. We looked for him until the hunt ended but it was not to be.

# *Chapter 3*

# The Big Splash

## Test Flying the "Kit Thing"

On March 25, 2002 at about nine o'clock in the morning I survived a serious "incident" with my kit built airplane. (I will explain this "incident" later).

It is the Kit Fox Model 5 that is shown in "The Potts Factor Versus Murphy's Law," with a buckled right main landing gear. (The company quit making the gear after several different gears had collapsed.)

After the "incident" the insurance company would not re-insure the aircraft unless the engine received a major overhaul. The reason being that the propeller had contacted the ground after the gear collapsed.

The price to overhaul Continental 0-200 engines was $12,500.00.

While trying to decide my best plan of action I found I could purchase a new Franklin four cylinder engine with sixteen (theoretically), more horsepower for $4,000.00 less.

So I sold the old 0-200 Continental engine and propeller and bought the new Franklin Engine and a new propeller.

The modern Franklin engines are made in Poland (or at least were until the company folded up, which added to the problems.)

All the Pollock Jokes in the world notwithstanding this joke is ultimately on me. (The polish guys call me "Stosh" anyway.)

I installed the new engine but could not get the R.P.M. to develop within about four hundred of what the manuals indicated it should produce.

I then put it on a trailer and hauled it to Challis, Idaho. I had Pete Nelson of Middle Fork Aviation try and help me find the reason I couldn't get the horsepower that the engine should produce.

We changed the induction system thinking it might not be getting enough air. This didn't help.

Carburetor was the next step. The engine was still under warranty and the factory said not to work on the carburetor, as this would void the warranty. Send it to them complete and they would fix the problem. We did, they didn't, and two different times might have gained 50 R.P.M. total.

About then I started to hear of other people that were having the same problem with their Franklin Engines. Not all, most were working great. Something was still radically wrong with mine.

I was flying the airplane back and forth to Challis for Pete Nelson to continue helping me but with the engine still running short of power. To haul it back and forth from where I live at Colson Creek to Challis is about two hundred and forty miles round trip with about forty of it over rough dirt roads. I just knew we would soon find the problem so I would have it working correctly.

My airstrip is pretty short, one thousand feet long, and with the engine producing much less power that it should have, take offs were marginal, but by taking off early in the morning when it was cool I was getting by o.k.

That is until this fateful morning that is etched very strongly in my memory bank. I did a preflight, warmed the airplane up and did my mag and mixture checks. Because leaning it to maximum power was very close to idle cut off, I richened the mixture a little with about 50 R.P.M. drop off.

I have a flag at the 500-foot or halfway point. If the tail was not solidly in the air at this point I would abort the take off. On prior take-offs, the plane would break ground at about six hundred feet. I would lower the nose, the airspeed would increase to best climb speed of about 68 M.P.H. and I would climb on out.

This day it lifted off O.K. but airspeed seemed to increase very sluggishly. About here was where I should have chopped the power and landed. I could have jumped on the brakes and ground looped if nothing else to keep from going over the bluff and into the river. As it turned out I found a very different, very violent way to get into the river.

At the west, down river end of the strip, the ground drops off about one hundred feet to the Salmon River. From the 600-foot mark, lift off point, to the edge of the bluff is only a few very short seconds. I had missed my chance to cut the power and get stopped so now I'm just hoping my airspeed will increase a little so I will have better control.

I flew over the edge of the bluff with only a few feet of altitude and I cannot continue in a straight line or drop the nose to pick up speed.

The river is a couple hundred feet wide with a grove of big Ponderosa trees on the far side. My only chance is a very gradual turn to the right and fly the river bends below the trees until I get enough altitude to get above them. I am on what is known as "the ragged edge of a stall"; the controls were very mushy. I had barely entered the very gradual turn when the aircraft stalled, dropping and hitting the river on the tip of the right wing.

I cannot tell you what happened for the next few moments. It was just very violently cart wheeling and flipping across the river and then it stopped.

I was under water and assumed I was upside down. I didn't know how deep the water was but knew I had to get out. I unbuckled my seat belt and couldn't move. My first thought was, "My back is broken!"

Then I realized I had to get out of the shoulder harness. As I undid it, the doors both popped open and the water poured through both doors carrying maps, cushions, headsets etc. into the river.

The aircraft is sitting upright in the middle of the river on its wheels! Airplane parts, wingtips, fabric, fiberglass and windshield are floating down the river. Somehow my handheld radio is still laying on the seat. I grab it and head for shore, not knowing if I can walk or if it's too deep and I will have to swim. Whew! It's only two or three feet deep and I can walk.

I had told Joy I would call her after I had taken off so she could telephone Pete in Challis and tell him I was on my way. I tried to call her, no answer, wet radio? I'm not sure.

About then I realize I've probably got broken fuel lines leaking fuel into the Salmon River, a designated Wild and Scenic River. With the combination of endangered salmon and contaminated water, I decided I'd better go back to the plane and shut off all fuel valves.

Just then, guys came running down from the bluff, hollering, "Are you OK?" "I am -- have a slight sore spot on my left elbow, that's all." One reason I was OK, I'd grabbed a riding helmet out of the saddle shed and put it on that morning, no idea why, the only time I have ever worn a helmet of any kind! Premonition? No idea, much of the tubing in the cabin around my head was bent or broken.

I waded back out, shut off all fuel lines but the header tank was below the water, couldn't tell about it. Waded back to the bank, tried Joy again, radio worked and I told her I had dumped the plane in the river and to call the sheriff, F.A.A., insurance company, the National Transportation and Safety Board, and Pete.

Some pilot must have been flying over and either saw it or heard us on the radio. I told her I had to go put the generator back on the backhoe so I could retrieve the "Kit Thing," (Pete's favorite name for it.) I had taken the generator off to haul to town for repairs. Not easy to replace with shaking hands. I got the tractor repaired, found long cables, chains, heavy ropes and took the tractor back to the edge of the bluff above the plane.

Called Joy again. She said Federal Aviation Administration and insurance agency did not want the plane moved until they could inspect and investigate. I went to a phone and explained to them the problems, if it was leaking fuel into a wild and scenic river, a whole bunch of us could be in trouble instead of only one of us.

They said, "Take pictures and get it out as best you can, and we'll get inspectors there as quickly as possible."

A few weeks after the "Kit Thing" and I had our bath in the river I received an email from a lady in Michigan that had been corresponding about her Franklin engine's lack of power. She had found out that, somehow, some of the Franklin camshafts had been ground for a different model engine and a few of us had received them! Cursed "Potts Factor," please be gone!

Joy called all our daughters to report my latest "misadventure." Our oldest daughter Kay called back that night with "Dad, if you need another chapter for your new book just make something up!"

Before Cliff Smart, the FAA inspector, arrived from Boise for his investigation, his supervisor called again to discuss the happenings. He asked me if it was an accident or an incident. I ask him for the parameters. His words were, "If all the control surfaces are intact and operable," it is an incident. I went to check. Elevator, and horizontal stabilizer, vertical stabilizer and rudder and flaparons, "All intact and operable." I called him back to report probably the most "Major incident" in the history of flight!

I am naturally, very happy to have survived it with no injuries but not happy with my decisions to keep flying it with its engine problems. The final irony of this story is this; the guy I sold the old 0-200 Continental engine to is still flying it with no problems! Also, Skystar Aircraft Company that builds the Kit Fox had declared bankruptcy so repair parts are now not available.

I have since taken quite a bit of verbal abuse from my pilot buddies. Probably the most polite, "Potts, there are easier ways to get your floatplane rating!"

## Go Cart and Airplane

This little story involves our M4Maule airplane 2058U, a couple of the neighbor kids here at Colson Creek, and me.

Jesse and Syringa Stark had a go-cart and would ride it around the neighborhood roads and around my airstrip roads. Occasionally they would venture onto the airstrip itself to do a few "Wheelies."

I had been flying somewhere one day and when I returned I let down to check my windsock and prepare to land. The timing for my landing and the time for a wheelie or two had occurred at the exact same time.

Now Colson Creek airstrip is only one thousand feet long with the approach "Thru the trees and over the river" and all contained within a narrow canyon. I kept circling as low as I could at about three or four hundred feet hoping they would see me.

Alas, I couldn't get their attention so just circled and waited till something changed so I could land. Finally, they left the runway and started back up the river on the road on the south side. I knew I would have nearly a minute to get down and land before they would be able to be back on the strip.

I cut around, dropped down over the river on final and saw they were approaching on the east upper end. I touched down and rolled up to the east end just as they cut back toward me.

I couldn't see the size of their eyes through the visors on their helmets but would guess they were somewhat past fully open! They flipped an immediate u-turn and headed home. I tied the plane down and stopped by their home on the way to mine.

Larry and Joni Stark, who were the dad and mom to these two, knew nothing about it. I ratted on the kids but we all knew the go-cart on the runway would have to end for safety sake for all concerned. It's tough being a kid not matter what our age!

# Fly with Bill Woods

*"The Old Man of the Mountains"*

THE TRAVELAIRE

Fly from Boise, Idaho, to any landing strip in our beautiful primitive area. Mountain flying a specialty for over twenty-five years. Vacation, hunting and fishing trips gladly arranged. We have radio contact with most of the dude ranches, packers and river runners in the back country.

Fly from Boise, the doorway to the land of memories, memories you'll never forget.

BILL WOODS

Route 1 Boise, Idaho

Phones: Office 343-3162 Home 939-6366

# The Boise Airstrip Story
# and How I Met Bill Woods

I have read stories written by long time pilots that flying consists of hours and hours of sheer boredom interrupted by moments of sheer terror.

This little tale will relate a flight that gave me a long enough moment of "sheer terror" to last several flying careers.

I was a fledgling pilot, maybe a couple hundred hours total time with a fresh private pilot certificate in my wallet.

Back then, the instruction for instrument flying consisted basically of covering the outside visibility up and letting you find out that you couldn't keep the airplane under control very long without outside the cockpit visibility or learning to "fly the gauges" or getting an instrument rating.

The minimal instrument training was primarily to teach you to keep the airplane out of the clouds and fog by scaring the HELL out of you. They did but I didn't realize how speedily a situation could develop to force you out of the mold.

I was flying a Cessna 150, 100 horsepower airplane from McCall, Idaho back to Wells, Nevada. It was late afternoon and December, just before Christmas.

I had dropped off one-half of my elk at Smoky Davis Meats in Boise to be processed into salami that I would share with my family and friends for the holidays.

I would land at what was then called Gowen Field, use a courtesy car to pick up my salami, get a motel room for the evening and fly on to Wells the next morning.

As I approached Boise from the north a pretty solid looking storm was approaching the area from the south and west.

I was over Boise and expecting landing instructions momentarily when the storm engulfed Gowen Field and they closed the field to VFR (visual flight rule) traffic. No problem, there were several landing fields and airstrips behind me in Boise that I had just passed over a few moments before. I would just turn back and land at one of them.

Bradley Field was the one I tried first but as I approached it the storm was getting pretty close. I changed my plan to land and hurried to land at Strawberry Glen. Once again the storm was getting too close for comfort.

O.K. I'll land at Stone Airstrip, better chance at borrowing a car there anyway.

Storm is getting closer but I'm on final and nearing the approach end of the runway landing to the east. Should get touched down o.k. before the storm engulfs the area, but the visibility disappeared. I probably had fifty feet of altitude and full flaps on the little plane.

A Cessna 150 doesn't climb very fast without flaps – much less with full flaps.

I tried to hold what I had for a second or two, thinking I'd get a glimpse of the ground. Nothing! I hit full power, tried to hold my heading, scared to retract any flaps. Try to remember what to do. Keep airspeed; keep the needle centered and the ball centered. Try to get some kind of climb, yah, a little climb, maybe fifty or one hundred feet per minute or so, but some, can't turn, don't remember what's ahead of me. I have no exact idea how long the "sheer terror" moment went on but it must have been from three to five minutes when my little bird poked her head out of the storm! Now, I drew probably my first deep breath as I turned back towards Floating Feather landing field, my last chance as it was getting dark and I was very low on fuel by now.

Floating Feather was a private field owned by legendary Idaho bush pilot, Bill Woods, known as the "Old Man of the Mountains".

He had operated a flying service for the previous twenty or thirty years from this spot. But now, he was not flying much anymore. The strip was a little narrow trail in the mud (it had been raining most of the week) and lined with big sagebrush.

At least I can see. I get it down safely but when I try to get out of the mud at the end of the strip my left main tire pulls away from the rim and I am stuck. Safe but stuck – o.k., I'll take it.

Trying to plan my next move, sleep in cramped seat, walk to highway and catch ride to town when I see car lights coming down the hill from a big pretty home on the bluff.

Big Cadillac car drives up and pretty lady rolls down window and asks if I need some help. She introduces herself as Mrs. Bill Woods. I tell my story, got to get to a motel and then get my tire fixed in the morning.

She said, "Bill will be home from work any minute, why don't you come stay with us and Bill can help you get the plane tire fixed in the morning."

Boy, from bad luck to good in only a few short moments!

Next morning Bill helped me get the tire and wheel off and we drove over to Stone Airport and got it fixed.

They asked me, "Did you go by the hanger last night in that storm?"

I sheepishly answered, "Yes."

They said, "Well we could hear you but we never saw anything."

Bill took me to Smokey Davis, picked up my salami and I left it at Stone airport. Back to Floating Feather, put wheel on, strip had dried a little and I got back to Stone, fueled up, loaded my salami and departed for Wells none the worse for wear, except for a few more grey hairs!

*"Chaining Up" for Winter Flying in the Rockies*

**Sent to me by airmail from trapper and mountain man, Brian Charles from Chamberlain Basin, Idaho.**

## Back to Bill Woods

The night I spent as a "drop in" guest of Mr. & Mrs. Bill Woods and daughter was a very enjoyable evening.

I will write my recollections of what Bill Woods told me that evening and morning just as I remember them.

A goodly portion of the events and stories were backed up by magazine and newspaper articles and stories that Bill would go to his bookcase and get for me to read. The newspaper articles were all from Boise papers and I assume were from the Boise Statesman. The magazine articles and feature stories were in the likes of Saturday Evening Post, Colliers, etc.

Other pilots that knew Bill far better than I did have different versions and memories of some of these events.

My apologies to everyone that remembers things differently than what I remember Bill telling me. It will be great reading either way and while I still have some semblance of a memory – I will pen it as such.

There will be no chronology or sequence of events and happenings – just things I remember him telling.

First, he said he had logged 52,000 hours of flying time. Other pilots say no, he couldn't have that much and their recollections are from 30,000 to 38,000 hours.

Just prior to my evening with Bill a major happening in the aviation world took place. In Switzerland, a flying legend named Hermann Geiger, known in Europe as "The Glacier Pilot" was killed in a midair collision while returning to land from a glacier rescue. He supposedly had logged 52,000 hours and Bill said, "Now I guess I have the most flying time of any living pilot."

At this time Bill was unable to pass his medical. I think he only had one airplane left – beautiful rust colored Stagger Wing Beach with turquoise upholstery.

To fly legally he had to have a licensed pilot fly with him. I'm not sure but I think he would take it up occasionally by himself.

All he said was, "What would they do – shoot me down?"

Bill said Walter Beech, the owner of Beech Aircraft Company and designer of the Stagger Wing called him one day many years before with a question. He asked Bill if he thought they could get the Stagger Wing in and out of Soldier Bar Airstrip for some publicity/advertising pictures.

Bill's answer: "I think so; I've had it in and out of there dozens of times already."

He told me he had a total of seventeen forced landings, most of them in the back country but that he had only been taken to the hospital once. Other pilots say no – more than that! Harold Dougal says more like twenty-one or twenty-two. Harold was doing lots of mountain flying during this period of time and wrote a book "Idaho Mountain Pilot."

Harold gave me permission to use a couple of paragraphs about "The Old Bold" pilot Bill Woods from his book. The next two paragraphs are verbatim from Harold's book:

One 'Old Bold' pilot I knew very well told me of an experience he had while flying in an old 6000 Travelair coming out of the Salmon River country one day and being trapped by bad weather and had no place to go safely, since a landing anywhere that he could see below would have been a disaster. He took a chance and pulled up into the clouds climbed up between nine and ten thousand feet and figured that from that point he should be over Boise valley in about one hour.

He continued on for exactly one hour, flying on a needle ball instrument and then let down. When he broke out of the clouds he was maybe 500 feet above Crouch, a small community in Garden Valley which is forty miles north of Boise and at an elevation of 3,157 feet. It is completely surrounded by mountains and the only way out then was to fly down the narrow canyon of the Payette River to Emmett, a town out in the valley."

He was one lucky boy that time. What he could not figure out was the wind and his ground speed. If I had done that, I'd still be imbedded in some pine trees on a mountain side! Thanks for letting me use this Harold.

The saying in pilot talk is, "There are old pilots and there are bold pilots, but there are no old, bold pilots." It should probably be changed to "There aren't many old, bold pilots!"

Bill told me he flew most of the supplies, tool, cement, lumber, roofing materials, pipe etc. for all the back country ranches and lodges in Central Idaho. He said he went eleven years straight averaging 3300 hours per year. He had a husband and wife mechanic team keeping his planes flying.

He had someone to load his plane while he rested or slept. He would leave Boise in the dark; arrive at his backcountry destination as enough daylight developed to land. Then continue all day, leaving the backcountry strips with just enough light to take off – fly back to Boise in the dark.

Mechanic crew would work on the plane and it would be loaded for his next days start. One of the forced landings happened right by his Floating Feather strip. Bill said he had a contract with the Fish and Game Department to fly cedar posts down into the Owyhee Desert for the construction of antelope traps.

He had hauled several loads with no problems. His first trip one morning though, didn't turn out so well. It was still pretty dark when he took off with the load that had been loaded during the night.

He said the plane went way further down the strip than usual. Finally lifted off very sluggishly, and then would not climb. He was out of strip and there was an alfalfa field just across the road to the left. He barely cleared the barbed wire fences and plopped it down in the hay field with minimal damage.

They unloaded the posts into a truck and somehow someone had miscounted and he had twice as many posts as he'd been hauling! If I remember right he said he'd been hauling 1600 pounds per trip in the Travelair and he had been loaded with 3200 pounds!

Another little tale of interest, there was an old Alaskan pilot that had come to Idaho and bought some land at the Mouth of Brush Creek on the Middle Fork of the Salmon River. His name was A.A. Bennett and the ranch was what is now the Flying B guest ranch owned by Flying Resort Ranches.

Bennett was getting pretty old and his eyesight was failing. It is rather common back there to spend a lot of time flying under a fog bank only a few hundred feet above the rivers. Sometimes the canyons are very narrow with not much maneuvering room.

Bill was flying the right hand side of the canyon below the fog when around a bend at the same altitude and traveling in the opposite direction came A.A. Bennett. Bill banked violently in a split second as Bennett's wing tip passed within a few feet of Woods' fuselage.

That afternoon Bill saw Bennett in Boise. He said, "Man that was a close one we had this morning!"

GUESS WHAT! Bennett hadn't seen him!

This same general area was the scene of one of Bills serious forced landings. I will relate it as told to me.

It was winter time – the engine blew on the Travelair. Up ahead was a small clearing between the trees in the ice and snow covered river. Bill put it down somehow with one wing bent only slightly backwards from a tree.

His two co-pilots, tiny dogs I think were wire haired terriors, and he went to the trees at the edge of the river where Bill built a fire for the evening. The next day Bill's buddy, Jim Larkin, came looking for Bill. Jim took a picture from above of the plane showing only the minimal damage of the bent wing.

He dropped a note for Bill to head down river to Pistol Creek or Indian Creek along with extra food and supplies. Jim would land and hike upriver to meet him. Bill said the snow was about three feet deep. He would throw the dogs a few feet ahead, snowshoe to them and then throw them on ahead.

The one little dog did not survive. It had started to snow again by the time he and Larkin met. Jim took a picture of Bill coming towards him through the falling snowflakes, as big as hen eggs, that is a classic. (Written up one of the magazine stories)

Jim was a lot younger than Bill but they kept track of each others flights and if either didn't make it to their intended destination – the other would be in the air looking.

Jim's wife Maxine was the secretary for the Idaho Outfitters Association for many years and one of our favorite people.

One year Jim was in the South – I think Georgia – flying a DC3 fighting forest fires. It was about April and the spring outfitters' meeting was going on in Grangeville.

We were partying one evening and decided to call Jim to tell him how much fun he was missing. When I talked to Jim I asked him when he would be coming home.

He said, "I have no idea, there is no employment down here and as soon as I dump a load of retardant and put out one fire – the natives just light another one so they have a job!"

Carl Kriley along with a couple of my old friends Floyd Posing and Bill Watson floated the plane down to Indian Creek airstrip the next spring. Bob Fogg, another old friend that flew for Johnson Flying Service out of McCall flew in a new engine in the Ford Tri Motor – the plane was repaired and Bill flew it out.

Carl wrote it up in his book "Salmon River Back Country Tales," Chapter 14, "Bush Pilots."

**FORD TRIMOTORS WERE FLOWN INTO MOST IDAHO BACK COUNTRY AIR STRIPS FOR MORE THAN 20 YEARS. HAROLD DOUGAL WAS PILOT. THIS TRIMOTOR OR ONE SIMILAR FLOWN BY BOB FOGG BROUGHT BILL'S ENGINE IN. PICTURE PROVIDED BY HAROLD DOUGAL.**

A twice a year, for many years, flight was for Bill to fly a Jersey milk cow in and out of the Root Ranch. In, in the spring and out in the fall! The Root Ranch was the scene and location of Bill's only trip to a hospital.

The ranch was owned at this time by a wealthy lady from the East. The ranch was for sale and she and some potential buyers hired Bill to fly them in to look at it. The trip was in August, the Root Ranch strip is at 5650 feet in elevation. Early morning, late evening take-offs, especially when loaded, are a must during the hot summer days.

Bill told his passengers that they would have to wait until it cooled down in the evening to take off for the flight back to Boise. They said no problem, so, Bill laid down in the shade of the wing and took a nap. About three o'clock in the afternoon guess what? Here come the passengers ready to go out.

Bill said, "No, remember I told you we have to wait until it cools off."

They kept badgering him. "What, aren't you the world famous bush pilot?" "Afraid of a little warm air?"

Bill said, "All right. Get in – I'll show you it won't fly."

Because of the wind direction he decided to take-off upstream. He said he pulled down to the furthest he could get, turned 45 degrees and watched the wind gusts coming towards him.

When an especially big gust was a couple hundred yards away Bill powered up in a rolling turn into the wind. He said he couldn't believe it. It lifted off and started to climb. About the time he got out of the last of ground effect and over the trees – climb quit happening but the terrain is rising!

Bill's last memory of what happened next was of having his head out the left hand window lifting first one wheel and then the other over tree tops. When he came to he was in the hospital in Boise.

He asked, "How are my passengers?"

"Pretty good. One broken leg, lot's of cuts and bruises."

Bill asked, "What's wrong with me?"

They answered, "Frostbite!"

He said he was still a little rummy but knew it was August – no frost possible – except when he went into the trees he had grabbed the fire extinguisher and pumped it into his boot and froze his foot!

He flew Marvin Hornbacks daughter's horse out of Pistol Creek or Indian Creek. I can't remember which. Harold Dougal said the plane was a Tri Motor Stinson. He said when he leveled out the horse somehow got some of the restraining ropes loosened and he had some excitement holding the horse back with one hand and flying with the other! (This was written up in one of the magazines.)

I will wind this down with two or three more "Airventures," as told to me by Bill that evening.

The old strip at Cabin Creek was up on the bench above where the present strip is. Where the strip is now was lots of trees. Bill was taking off, had cleared the ground, but needed a little more power. He leaned the mixture a little but the mixture control came out in his hand shutting the engine totally down. Yup, into the trees with a much bent airplane.

This is a really sad one. During World War II, Bill said the government asked him to be an instructor in B17's out of Gowen Field. He flew and instructed for a short time, but said he hated the B17's. Too many problems – mainly catching fire. Bill told them – I quit!

A short time later, one of his friends was instructing in one, it caught fire, he either couldn't get to Gowen Field or was closer to Floating Feather and tried to get in there. As he came over the end of the strip a wing burnt off, fell on Bills hanger, burnt it and three uninsured airplanes up plus killing his friend and the student.

Bills words, "Even after quitting, I still couldn't get away from them!"

The last story from my old memory bank was (I think), the last flight of his beloved Travelair.

He was flying construction materials into Mackay Bar. The Travelair had a problem with the left rudder hanging up and not neutralizing when you released it. He said it was not a major problem. You kicked the right rudder and it would release. He'd fly all day and the husband and wife mechanics would try to fix the problem.

No time to waste test flying it. You tested on the paying trips. Bill had it loaded with ¾" sheets of plywood stacked nearly to the headliner.

He would be landing upriver at Mackay Bar. You came upriver, the South Fork of the Salmon comes in on your right, and you

**BILL WOODS, IN COVERALLS, WITH FRIENDS AT HIS FLOATING FEATHER AIRPORT WEST OF BOISE. THE PLANE IS A STINSON 6000 MOD "U" TRIMOTOR. WOODS, WHO CALLED HIMSELF OLD MAN OF THE MOUNTAINS, ALWAYS FLEW WITH TWO WIRE HAIR TERRIERS. THIS IS THE PLANE THAT BILL FLEW MARVE HORNBACKS DAUGHTER'S HORSE OUT IN. THANKS TO RANDY WOODS AND HAROLD DOUGAL FOR THE USE OF THIS PICTURE.**

make a 90 degree left turn to line up with the strip. Bill come in, made his left turn to line up, rudder stuck, no problem, kick hard on right rudder and it releases, correct? Wrong!

Airplane continues in left turn, across river and into mountain side with great force. The left wing hit first which obviously saved Bill's life. If the aircraft impact would have been direct from the front the many sheets of plywood would have crushed Bill, seat, engine and all. As it was, it catapulted Bill right out the side of the airplane and down the mountainside. Only damage to Bill was it tore his overalls when he went through the side of the airplane! Boat came across the river and picked him up – basically none the worse for wear.

They took the plane apart, got it to the road up to Elk City, loaded it on a little semi and hauled it to the top. Bill said it was in such bad shape from the crash and the ride up the mountain from dragging on rocks and trees he just decided to give up on it.

A wild story, a wild life!

Bill said he went 11 years straight and banked over $100,000 each year after all expenses, airplane rebuilds, etc. That was when a dollar had some value!

One of the highlights of my life, the night I dropped in on Bill Woods and heard these stories!

Bill wrote an article that was published in the Idaho Department of Aeronautics flyer called "The Rudder Flutter". This was sent to me by Dick Waite and I think is a fitting ending to my story regarding one of Idaho and the worlds' early day airmen. The name of the article is "IF I COULD WRITE." (If I could write like Bill did I would be very happy!)

## If I Could Write

If I could write, I'd write of summertime and early morning flight, of pink-tinged mountain peaks with their green fir robes topped with caps of ermine white, of silver rivers far below winding thru multi-colored canyons, of the soft gray stratus clouds dissolving before the suns first bright rays. I would try to tell of the pilot's highway, wide as the world itself, of the peace and eternal solitude and the deep sense of adventure while gliding thru shadowy corridors among the ever changing Cumulus clouds, and of a motor's roar; breathing the cold clean air high above the earth-bound dust and smoke as the remote earth, so very far below, slowly breaks into a million sunlit and shadowy patterns.

If I could write I'd try to tell you of midday flight when the sun's hot breath has awakened every devilish air current, of a plane being tossed around like a loose leaf before winter's early winds. I would describe that awful feeling of aloneness-the chill terror-and how mere seconds creep by like old and worn out years, as those wind devils slam your plane toward bleak canyon walls, your controls as dead as yesterdays dreams. I'd write of the quick panic you try to hold away as you wait for that life saving cushion of air that you can only hope is trapped beside the canyon wall. I guess I'd even try to make you feel the deep inside hurting of the clatter of an over-worked, over-heated motor fighting for precious altitude while those demanding down-drafts are pulling you down, down, down. I might even tell you how little and insignificant you feel when a thousand crazy air currents have grabbed your plane and are shaking it much like a hungry cur shakes a meatless bone, of broken tiedown ropes and a heavy load of loose freight floating up tight against the ceiling as the plane itself falls faster than the pull of gravity, and of the chaotic thoughts within your mind while you wait for the solid air and wonder if man-made wings of wood and fabric can take the shock.

If I could write of winter flights when the deep white snows have hidden and locked away every meadow and glade where-in the plane could find a haven, of black storms chasing one another at mile a minute speeds, of sudden clouds pregnant with snow, dragging their bloated bellies along the ground, hiding every familiar landmark, and of flying in blizzards when the visibility is less than a hundred feet an hour seems like a million. I'd write of the dull, clumsy, dead weight of a plane loading up with ice and of the anguished gasp of a radial motor breathing only wet and freezing air. I might even try to tell you of how it feels to be boxed in by the storms, of the helplessness that permeates your whole being while you are using all of the skill, cunning and knowledge that you have accumulated in a lifetime of flying just to hold death away a little longer. I'd write of how you will look at your hands on the controls and marvel at the wonderful pieces of flesh and blood mechanism that they are and wonder just how much longer they will have the life and power to obey the commands of your brain.

I would also tell of how your heart swells to almost a breaking point when you finally get thru and how good the cold clean ground feels beneath your feet, ground that only moments before you thought that you would never again feel and walk on.

If I could write, why most of all I would write of how good human companionship is after one of these flights, of how a baby's cry, a child's laughter, a woman's smile or friendly touch is worth more than the tinkle of golden coins in a blind beggar's cup. But what I would never hope to write about is that inconceivable pull, that ever constant compulsion, stronger and more demanding than steel cables that persists in taking you back and back, as though your soul were a veritable fragment of the air you breathe and fly in. Of that I could never write, for I do not have the humble understanding that belongs to God alone.

NOTE: The foregoing was written by Bill Woods, the "Old Man of the Mountains," who had flown over twenty nine thousand hours among the Sawtooth Mountains of Idaho's Primitive Area. He had flown horses, cows, hogs, mules, tractors, even complete lodges together with all their equipment, power plants and thousands of hunters and fishermen into these mountains, in winter and summer over about thirty years of constant flying.

## DO'S AND DON'TS ON MOUNTAIN FLYING

**By Bill Woods**

Idaho has some of the most beautiful mountain ranges in the world. There are hundreds of lakes located in these peaks of eight thousand feet altitude and up, so exquisite in their beauty they will take your breath away.

Here also are the primitive rivers, still unspoiled by civilization, rushing along as they have for thousands of years. Here, too, is one of the greatest fish and game countries left in the United States. It is all yours, the airplane pilot's heaven on earth, just for the taking. But before you rush in to enjoy this primitive paradise, stop for a moment and let's talk this mountain flying over a little just for the sake of a little common sense.

The following advice is based on considerably more than a thousand flights in our Primitive Area and may be of some help to the amateur mountain pilot regardless of the amount of hours he may have tucked away beneath his flying belt.

1. First and foremost do not consider, for one minute, flying the back country unless you have at least one hundred and fifty hours and are proficient in slow flight.
2. Know your airplane. Do not take a ship into this territory that will not take off and land in a minimum distance. It takes a lot of experience to handle a hot airplane in this region.
3. **Remember** that for each thousand feet you are above sea level, it will increase your take off run approximately twenty-five per cent and your landing speed two percent with a longer run due to your increase in landing speed.
4. Know the field you are going into. Check with experienced mountain pilots if possible—know the altitude, the length, and whether it is a one way field. Most of these fields are one way and on many it is impossible to go around if you overshoot.
5. Check your weather and stay out of doubtful or bad weather.
6. Make your trips in the early morning hours. The air, as a rule begins to get bad around 10:00 a.m., grows steadily worse until about 4:00 p.m., then gradually improves until dark.
7. Stay out of the mountains if the wind is over twenty-five miles per hour.
8. Keep your airplane as light as possible. **Do not** carry one pound of needless weight.
9. Route your trip over valleys whenever possible and study your charts thoroughly—watch your compass and don't get lost.
10. Maintain as much altitude as possible at all times.

11. Hit all ridges at an angle so you can turn away if you hit a down draft. After you cross the ridge head directly away from it.

12. Expect the wind to be changing constantly in the mountains. Don't rely on cloud shadows for wind direction. If you can't gain altitude on one side of a canyon, try the other—if there is no improvement there, ride the center but under no circumstances head up any canyon or valley without sufficient altitude and room to turn around—the grade of the canyon may climb faster than your airplane.

13. Keep that flying speed in down drafts. Don't get panicky, just remember that air does not go through the ground—a ground cushion of air will always be there unless below the top of the timber—the stronger the down draft, the greater velocity it will have when it changes direction.

14. Remember you will not have a horizon to check the attitude of your plane once you begin to let down in the mountains. Watch your airspeed, your altimeter and a good rate of climb is worth its weight in gold.

15. On landings, come in upstream whenever possible and with the airplane at minimum speed with power. If the plane is settling too fast, add more power; if it isn't coming down fast enough, cut a little power, but do not make power off approaches—**They Are Dangerous.** When you are sure you will hit the runway near the end, chop the power and make a full stall landing. These fields are **short.**

16. Do not drag into mountain fields with a low approach as a down draft has everything its own way under these conditions. If you feel doubtful about your approach, get out while you are still high and **do not** go into land until you are satisfied. Do not go out of sight of the field on your approach if possible as another ship may start a take off. If this is necessary due to the terrain, circle the field until the pilots on the field definitely know you are going to land.

17. Do not make turns to land at low altitude. Go far enough from the field to turn so execution can be made at a safe altitude. This also gives you time to get the feel of slow flight while coming in. **Do not** park your airplane on the runway. This is not only extremely poor air manners but endangers a fellow pilot by robbing him of much needed landing space. AND if you find turbulent air when you let down in the canyons, come on home—this type of air has no respect for you, regardless of your experience and ability.

18. Use common sense on take offs. If the air is bad or if you have a tail wind, wait it out. Remember none of these fields are long enough to land again once you have left the ground —let the airplane use all the runway it needs as long as runway is available, then it will be flying when it leaves the ground. Do not pull it off until you are sure of flying speed unless you run out of runway.

**19. You can gain extra take off speed by making your turn at the end of the field a good fast taxi speed and opening your throttle as the plane swings around to line up with the runway. Practice this maneuver with an instructor on a good standard airport.**

Under ordinary circumstances you can expect the wind to be blowing upstream in the mornings and afternoons as the air and terrain heats up and downstream in the evenings as it cools off. Cold air is heavy and goes down hill while hot air is light and goes up. Expect to find down drafts over all streams as they cool the air. Know the wind if possible; watch the topography and with a little common sense you can tell where the updrafts and downdrafts will be. Remember air is like water and follows the contour of the land it is flowing over. Use the updrafts to help you gain altitude but do not fly a ship in this territory that does not have a ceiling sufficient to get you out without help from the updrafts.

Always remember that you are flying in a huge and very sparsely populated territory. If you have an accident, it may be some time before anyone knows about it. You will be landing on fields where there is no one to help you in case of trouble and it is a long walk out. Don't take chances and don't get rattled.

Before you fly into this territory practice short field landings with power, upwind, downwind, and crosswind. Be sure you can set your plane down on a fifty foot spot, not once in a while, but every time. Take maps with you—know your route and the weather. Let someone know when you are going, the route you are going to use, and when you will be back. Do not fly into any basins or valleys at high altitudes that do not have an outlet where you can get out in a hurry in case of downdrafts. Remember winds of from forty miles per hour and up are common at ten thousand feet altitude. Carry enough gas to make your complete round trip plus fifty percent more. You will need it more times than not and, above all, fly the airplane every second, don't let it fly you. You cannot make mistakes in this territory.

**WRITTEN IN 1950.**
**THANKS TO RUDDER FLUTTER AND DICK WAITE FOR THE USE OF THIS ARTICLE.**

## *Chapter 4*

# More Shadow Memories of Stan & Joy

In the spring of 1990, Joy and I drove to San Diego to attend the Foundation For North American Wild Sheep Convention.

On our way back we stopped in Las Vegas to see my sister Marlene Huebert and her husband Chuck and our niece Marci and nephew Cory. They were raising German Shorthaired Pointers and had just weaned a litter of 10 puppies. They asked us if we would like a pup and we said yes.

Now we had also just inherited an old dog-named Ringo. His master, Bill Bilger, had died and Ringo was basically a man's dog, and wouldn't stay home with Bill's widow Lee. He would come across the creek to our place and stay all day. Lee would come get him and take him home but back he would come. We told Lee we would love to have Ringo if that would work better for her and she agreed to it.

On our way to the convention we had gone thru Buhl, Idaho and left Ringo with our daughter Kay Black and husband Jerry, grandson Jay and granddaughter Jeny. Now, on our way home we were wondering how to get the old dog Ringo to tolerate the new four-pound bundle of energy! When we drove into their yard they came out to meet us with the sad news that Ringo had ran in front of the pickup and been killed. It had just happened a few hours before we arrived. Jay had just finished burying him.

The pup bonded with both of us, was housebroken immediately and was with one or the other of us constantly. Hence the name Shadow. Full name Lucky, Three Spot, Hugh Rob, Shadow, Von Wiebold, Potts. He'd found a home.

## Of Steelhead, Elk, and Heat Exhaustion

He loved to go fishing and would point the big steelhead out in the water. While I was running the outfitting business in the mountains Shadow would stay home with Joy. He figured out if he followed a car or pickup with fishing poles they might let him help fish.

Joy couldn't make him stay home and it was terribly frustrating for her to go after him three or four times a day. I wasn't able to take the time right then to break him of leaving. It would be a couple of months before I would have any time to work with him.

We decided to see if we could give him away. We placed an ad in the paper, but the only calls were people with funny accents, and Joy didn't think they were interested in him as a pet.

After hunting season ended and I got the gear put away and the horses and mules on winter pasture I would now have some time for the dog re-training project.

The first day he followed some fisherman upriver and I followed him. They stopped to fish the Clam hole a couple miles from home. When he looked up and saw my old brown pickup drive up he actually went out in the water a few feet and laid down on a flat rock with his head between his paws as if he was trying to hide. He knew he was in trouble.

**THE WORLDS GREATEST CAT POINTER-note the terrified cat!**

I had come prepared for the training session with a double leather strap about two inches wide and two feet long. It really cracked when you applied it to the shoulders or rump of a horse or mule so I figured it would do the same on Shadow. The loud crack, as the second strap cracked against the first was an attention getter.

I went down to the fisherman and told them I would be taking him home and if he came back to just tell him to go home and he would. I wasn't sure how successful the training session would be.

I called him and we climbed up the hill to the pickup. I turned it around and drove back toward home around a bend in the road. I got the leather strap and paddled him about six times on the butt all the while reinforcing the punishment with the "Bad Dog," talking to. I repeated the procedure about six more times on the trip home.

Upon my arrival at the house I left him in the pickup to think about the previous few minutes. I went in the house and told Joy how I had handled his training. Now we would let him come in the house and we would both treat him very kindly with no harsh words. It took! He never left home again except to chase bears, raccoons and deer out of the yard.

He would tree a bear or raccoon and then stand upright with one foot on the tree and point them without barking! This made it pretty hard, to find the tree in the dark, if he treed them very far out of our

**A SUCCESSFUL CHUKAR CHASE**

yard. Sometimes I just wouldn't find him and he would come back on his own after an hour or so.

When he was younger I would take him to the mountains while cutting trails, setting up the hunting camps, cutting firewood, lake-fishing trips etc.

On one of these trips, on a nice spring day, at Cradle Creek Camp, some elk cows and baby calves came around the mountain about 200 yards above the camp. Shadow decided to go up and harass them a little. When he got about halfway up to them, one of the cows came out of the bunch and took after him on a dead run, her ears were laid back.

Naturally he came to me to save him! Fortunately for both of us the cow decided she had done her job before she got all the way to us, good thing, or else "McMutt" and I would have both been in trouble.

Another year Pat Hendren and I were setting Cradle Camp and cutting firewood with the six foot "Misery Whips." This camp is in the Frank Church Wilderness area and no chainsaws or power equipment is allowed.

The year before I had "Requisitioned" some of the firefighter's paper sleeping bags out of their dumpster. The bags worked well for summer campouts and I took one for myself on this trip.

Unbeknownst to me I had half of a sleeping bag! Top or bottom

**THE TOUGH LIFE OF A HUNTING DOG!**

didn't matter. I laid some saddle pads on a canvas tarp and laid the half bag on top. It was a cold August night. I would wake up cold and you know who would be snuggled into and under my cover! They don't call them "Shorthairs" without a reason! It was a long night because Shadow had our half sleeping bag a lot more of the time than I did.

Back then he was young and in good shape. Still the 18-mile trip would wear him out, mostly because he would triple or quadruple it by chasing pine squirrels and chipmunks, and pointing grouse and chukar. I would take several quarts of water for him to drink and to pour on him to cool him off.

One especially hot August day going down Grassy, about a three-mile walk with no shade, Shadow became fatigued and dug a hole under sagebrush for shade. I gave Shadow another drink of water and poured some water on his back but he wouldn't come out. I tried to pull him out but he was nearly delirious and bit me!

A neighboring outfitter Dave Melton and one of his guides, Brad Patterson, were with me. We were in major trouble, as somehow I had to get him on down the mountain to shade and more water that was still about a mile away.

We finally got him out of his hole under the sagebrush and I got on my mule and had Brad hand him up to me. I had to try to get him down to the cold water at the North Fork of Stoddard Creek. He weighed 75 or 80 pounds then and balancing him on the front of my saddle was definitely not easy.

When I got to a switch back about 400 yards above the Creek I got off with Shadow and headed straight down to the creek leaving Dave and Brad to bring my mule and the pack string down using the trail.

A few minutes of him laying in the creek and lapping the cold water revived him and we were able to go on the next hour or so to camp.

Another trip, I had taken Shadow with two of my good mules, Doc and Ben. We went up to the Nolan Lookout area to glass for rams prior to the start of sheep season. We had been camped a day or two and one morning I decided to leave the mules tied up for a few hours, while Shadow and I descended a ridge about one thousand feet to get a different look at a distant mountain.

**HEATHER AND JOHN HOPKINS AND THE LAP DOG!**

Around noon, not being able to spot any rams, we headed back to the mules. As we got closer I could hear them braying and screaming like they were in mortal pain. Upon our arrival the mules were bucking and screaming around the trees they were tied to. They were literally covered with horseflies and being nearly eaten alive!

I got my camp rolled up but then, how to saddle the mules and pack up was the interesting and dangerous problem.

The ground was covered with burnt logs and limbs from one of the many forest fires. I would blanket and saddle a mule as he was bucking and kicking around trees and over the logs and limbs. I was lucky I didn't get knocked down below one and get stomped to death.

I got the packs kind of thrown at the sides of the mules and got them pigtailed together. We all took off at a dead run down the trail trying to get away from the horseflies.

After a couple of miles, and a drop in elevation of a couple thousand feet, we left the horseflies behind and I was able to redo my packs and we continued at a little more leisurely pace.

Unfortunately, in the race to out run the horseflies I hadn't been able to stock up on water for Shadow and now we had about four miles to get to the river with no creeks between us and the river.

I only had about a quart of water and it was mid August, little shade after all the recent forest fires and it was getting late in the afternoon and well over 100 degrees.

We got down to the switchbacks above the river and I gave Shadow the last of the water as he was badly in need of it. He would get in the trail in front of me and lay down under whatever bit of brush or weeds that had some shade and rest so I couldn't get around him.

After three or four switchbacks he decided he could go straight down the mountain to the next switchback, find a little shade and lay down to wait for me and get a little more rest that way.

When we were about 100 yards above the river I tied up the mules and got a hold of his collar and we went to the river. I was afraid he would just jump in and he would either drown or drink too much or drink too fast and die. I slowly got him re-hydrated enough that I could go back for my mules and we went on home to tell our story. (Another wild day while moving west!)

One time Shadow killed some kind of dumb bird on our deck at the house. Joy felt bad and gave him the "Bad Dog" talking to.

Some time later, I took Shadow chukar hunting, I could not figure out what was wrong. He wouldn't work, wouldn't even look at them as they were running all round him. When I came home and told Joy, she gave me the dead bird on the deck story.

He was so smart that even, with his over powering pointer breeding; he figured he shouldn't even hunt chukar for me. It took quite a few hunts to convince him it was o.k.

## Shadow the Sled Dog

One winter a couple of our down river friends, Heidi Leavett and Rob Rishor, decided to put together a sled dog team. They had several hounds that they used to hunt mountain lions with and they bought Shadow a harness and added him to their dog team which included a Husky.

They had built a cart that could have wheels or runners for whatever the conditions warranted. They had to send someone (usually me), ahead to watch for lion tracks crossing the road or chukars. It would have been quite a wreck with Shadow pointing a chukar, just as the lion dogs headed over the bank on a fresh lion track.

**Heidi Leavett on cart-Rob Rishor and Stan Potts wait for a wreck!**

We made several trips up and down the river road. It was great fun with only minimal problems.

## The Dogfight That Ruined Shadow

One spring day I was at the hangar working on the airplane. I heard dogs barking and a dogfight start. I ran out and a little pickup with three dogs in it had gone by and all the dogs had jumped out.

Shadow was in the middle of a three-to-one dogfight. One dog was like a small Poodle; another of medium size cow dog type and the third was a big Rottweiler and Yellow Lab cross.

As I ran towards the melee Shadow was doing the best he could against the big dog but with the two smaller dogs biting his underside he would have to turn the big dog loose. Finally the big dog headed for their pickup and jumped in. Shadow grabbed him by the hind leg and testicles and nearly ripped everything off as he jerked him back out of the pickup.

I got there about then and it was a pretty bloody mess. Shadow had fang punctures through his skull plus one eye was badly injured. With all the straining he had ruptured himself on both sides.

In order to repair the ruptures we had to take him to a specialist in Pocatello, Idaho (which is a five hundred mile round trip). He had to be neutered, and then one side repaired and healed before the other side could be fixed. The big dog had to have one leg removed and died a few days later.

Shadow gained about 20 pounds after being neutered and could never go to the mountains again.

## False Guilt and Sympathy Pains

One year Joy had to have a worn-out hip replaced with a hip transplant.

She had it done in Boise and a couple of days after the operation, began training to use the crutches -- how to go up and down stairs, etc. With that behind us, we came home. It is a six or seven hour drive and Shadow was with us.

Because of the crutches and slow tender movements, he knew something was wrong with Joy.

The first night, Joy got out of bed and started to stand up. She let out a scream. "Stan, something is wrong! I can't stand the pain!"

I called the EMT's and an ambulance. It takes an hour and a half for an ambulance to get down here into the canyon. Then it was very hard to maneuver the stretcher down the stairs. Joy was in horrific pain, with a long, bouncy ride to the hospital, the first seventeen over dirt roads winding along the roudy Salmon River.

At the hospital in Salmon, the x-rays showed the femur had broken where they had installed the new hip socket. No wonder Joy was in pain!

They life flighted her back to Boise, where she would be in the hospital a week and have three cables placed around the femur. (It's quite fun getting her through airport security nowadays!)

Shadow and I returned home to wrap up the place so we could leave for Boise. He of course, could not have known about Joy's life flight to Boise, he simply knew it was me and Shadow alone. I cleaned up the house and started getting some breakfast, when I realized I hadn't seen Shadow.

After a long search, I found him in the doghouse that he hated and had never used since a few hours his first night home as a puppy several years before.

He wouldn't come out and had this mournful look on his face.

I finally coaxed him out and he proceeded to LIMP to the house!

Somehow, he felt her suffering was his fault, and because she was hurt, he would do part of the limping for her!

## Shadow's Near-Human Compassion

In one of my bent airplane fiascoes, Shadow exhibited a trait that to this day leaves Joy and I wondering if he was really a dog or a four legged mind reader.

I had landed our M4-MAULE airplane on about eight inches of hard crusted snow one evening here at Colson Creek.

As I was nearly rolled to a stop, the main landing gear wheels broke through the snow crust and the plane tipped up on it's nose. The propeller bent backward and the plane slid eighteen feet on it's nose.

Some guys helped me tip it onto the wheels and I towed it to the hangar with the pickup.

Now, Shadow loved that airplane. It had a wide cargo door on the right side and was low enough to the ground that he could easily jump in. I installed an eyebolt in the center to hook him to so he could look out either side or put his head between the front seats to see where were were headed and to watch me fly. He would be badly bent out of shape if he didn't get to go flying, but fortunately, he had not been aboard for this less-than-text-book landing.

I put the bent-prop plane in the hangar and dragged on back to the house to tell Joy of my misfortune.

Shadow somehow picked up on my words, voice, inflection or demeanor that all was not well in Pottsville.

Now, Shadow had a spectacular menagerie of stuffed animals including monkeys, camels, skunks, bears, and dolls of various shapes and sizes. Our log home has three levels, and he kept a supply of toys scattered on all three levels. He knew each one, and would go find them by name wherever they were located.

That night I hit the sack early, gloom like a black cloud above my bed. Shadow went into action, and finding ALL of his toys, he laid them along my side of the bed.

He somehow knew I needed some cheering up and did his best by sharing his treasures with me.

If you had wanted to see a grown man cry, that would have been the time to have been around.

## Shadow Stories by Joy

As Stan has told, we acquired Shadow in kind of a fluke, from our brother-in-law Chuck Huebert. Chuck's female German Shorthair had 10 pups, this her first litter. Chuck had sold all the females for top dollar, but had six males with four not spoken for. So he just gave us the papered pup.

We brought him home from Vegas, starting out with him in a box on the back seat of the car and before long, I had this long legged speckled pup curled in my lap and from then on he always thought he was a lap dog.

When we got home with Shadow and not having Ringo, like we'd planned, we put him in the doghouse with a clock to keep him company. About midnight we couldn't stand any more howling and brought him in the house. He promptly curled up by Stan's side of the bed and that's where he slept from then on.

I guess coming from such a large litter Shadow would eat about anything and quickly. One day I found this very strange looking string of doggy do. It had whole pieces of nuts, aluminum foil and some kind of paper plus other ugly things. We found he had eaten a couple candy bars from Stan's pickup and had swallowed them both without much chewing.

He also ended up staying with Vet Lady and family for a few days because he had eaten so many cherries, seeds and all. That he was so impacted he had to have an enema plus laxatives.

"Now you share like a big guy," was all I had to say and it didn't make any difference what it was, food or toys he'd share.

One of those days he must have been extra hungry because when the neighbors dog started to eat out of his dish, he got his extra dish and put it down beside her, like, "Here, that's mine you eat this."

Toys were big on his list and there for awhile I'd bring him a toy when we went somewhere, until he had a big collection. He had a monkey he was very fond of. We always told him to be nice to toys.

It was spring and Stan was rototilling the garden. He called me to come look. There, wrapped up in the tiller was Monk, with bites in him. All we could think was Shad had played a little too rough with Monk and didn't want us to see, so he buried him.

He also killed a raccoon and buried it in our neighbor's garden, which gave Dianne quite a start when she dug it up. His favorite of all time toy was a Barney character from children's T.V. whenever anyone came to visit, the first thing he grabbed was Barney to show off. In fact Barney is buried with him.

Bears would come down to the orchards in the fall. Shadow took great delight in chasing them up trees or whatever was around for them to climb. All of the trees large enough to hold a bear have claw marks on the bark. One especially exciting chase involved a raccoon, Shadow, a bear and me.

Shad and I were alone about 3:00am when Shadow started to growl and out the doggie door he went. I could hear a great commotion up on the deck so went up to investigate. Shadow had a large raccoon "treed" on the top of a log upright, I called him off and back down stairs to bed we went.

Next thing I know Shadow is outside under a large ponderosa tree by the deck, looking up. Up the stairs I went, grabbing a very weak flashlight. Going out on the deck under the limbs of the tree I shone the light down on Shad and told him there was no raccoon around.

Next thing I heard was swoosh by my head and shining the very weak light right in the eyes of a very large bear. I started backing away toward the door of the house saying "OH SHAD! BEAR!" Shadow was probably thinking "I bring them to her and she never does anything with them."

There are so many stories, but time and space does not allow. Shadow was a great dog and friend and even two years after losing him, we still miss him.

During the winter of 2004, Shadow started developing a cough. We took him in for a check up but nothing could be pinpointed as to the cause. The cough kept getting worse so we took him back in for a complete checkup and the chest x-rays found one lung nearly full of cancer so our old buddy's life came to an end. A sad day in Pottsville! Shadow was a great dog.

# Chapter 5

## Windstorms and Near Casualties

Violent windstorms have played a large role in my life, from major excitement to absolute terror and everything in between. Property damaged and destroyed has also figured into the mix.

A year or so after Joy and I got married we decided to try raising sheep. Our plan was to buy aged ewes, breed them, lamb them out and sell the pairs in the late spring.

We bought the sheep herd over in Opal, Wyoming and decided because we were going to be lambing them in the early spring with cold inclement weather that we would need a lambing shed. We bought the lumber and canvas for the roof and constructed a shed 150' long by 12' wide, with 4 foot panel pens along both sides and a 4 foot walkway in the center. It worked really well but now as they say "for the rest of the story".

We were nearly done lambing (fortunately), with very few sheep left in the shed, when a violent windstorm came out of the west. It took our beautiful lambing shed and rolled it like a barrel into our creek. All that was left was a giant mess of splintered boards and canvas to clean up and burn. Oh yes, we lost money on the sheep when we sold them. Story of our lives, lose money on every deal and make it up in volume!

When we were ranching in Clover Valley, Nevada we found out it had a bad reputation for HUGE windstorms. There had been several people killed from winds. Usually they were out in an open field with a team and hay wagon and the wind would tip the wagons over on them.

About a year after we bought the ranch we had our first chance to witness the fury of the wind first hand. There was an old barn that had been used for the teams of horses. It would hold about four or five teams with mangers for their hay and racks on the walls for the harnesses. The resident bird herd consisting of guinea fowl and peacocks roosted in the rafters of the barn. I had a two year old registered quarter horse stallion named Kenny Dawson in the horse corral next to the barn. The corral was fenced with railroad ties and stood about six foot high. Just outside of the corral, I had my one horse trailer parked next to a five hundred gallon gasoline tank on a stand.

Our ranch was located about three miles east of a mountain range that towered over five thousand feet above the valley floor. In theory, that should stop or at least slow down any wind from the west, right? Wrong! It just somehow multiplied the winds velocity.

Usually there was a visual warning of small to large cumulus type clouds that gathered over the mountains and part way down the mountainside. It was called by the locals the "Wind cloud on the mountains", and there was no mistaking it.

**PAINTED FOR US BY LONG TIME FRIEND AND CLIENT, SID BOURBOULIS**

The following events transpired on one of these mornings of the "Wind cloud". First the wind came up with enough velocity to encourage, no, drive me to the house.

Our home was a ten room two story house and the west side of the house was of poured concrete walls. The wall was about ten feet high and one foot in thickness. Someone had survived one or more of the Clover Valley breezes and had incorporated their memory of same into the home construction.

Our kitchen window looked north toward the barn and corrals and I was standing at the sink and watching the devastation unfold.

First, the gas tank blew over onto my horse trailer as it tipped over.

Secondly, the wind actually picked up my stallion that weighed eight or nine hundred pounds and draped him over the six foot corral fence.

Thirdly, the barn disintegrated and the sky was full of flying lumber, Guinea fowl and Peacocks and Peahens. About then for lack of anything better, I said, "Blow, you son-of-a-bitch, BLOW!"

Sure enough! A broken 2"x12" hit the kitchen window and scattered broken glass all over the kitchen. That was nearly fifty years ago and when I am tempted to utter similar words of encouragement to a situation, those words or results usually surface.

The stallion fell back into the corral so I can't actually say it blew him over the fence. Later, we actually found dead peacocks and Guinea hens over one mile away from where the barn had stood.

The second major wind was a few years later. We had started irrigating the ranch with side roll sprinklers and were trying to figure a system of anchoring them when they were not in use. I had chained corral poles about 20' long across each end of the quarter mile lines. Then I had driven steel posts in the ground and chained the pipes to them.

It was late November and I had been working for a neighboring rancher, Homer Jaynes. He had contracted to plant several hundred acres of wheat grass seed for the adjacent ranch owned by Darrell and Deena Weeks.

We had finished the planting and were short cutting through my field back to the road when the wind hit us. We were between two of the staked down sprinkler lines when the wind pulled them apart. The torque of the pipes when the steel posts pulled out and the poles broke actually catapulted them towards us like harpoons or arrows. You kind of hoped that your number hadn't come up while this was going on.

Homer Jaynes was the Mormon Bishop at that time. I don't know if he had any extra pull with the big guy upstairs or not but we survived.

The same windstorm tipped Darrell Weeks pivot sprinkler over and totally destroyed it along with his new equipment shed.

Our side roll sprinklers ended up all tangled in the barbed wire fence at the east end of our field three quarters of a mile away. Not a fun job to untangle and repair!

## Idaho Windstorms

In the past few years here at Colson Creek and back in the mountains more wind storms have occurred, several that I have been involved with.

Some of these storms were just a hairbreadth, a few inches or a few moments from disaster.

The first major one was about 1990. We hadn't built the new house yet and our only facilities, for our outfitting operation, were a couple of small house trailers about twenty five feet long, horse corrals constructed from ten foot long metal panels and a couple of canvas tents with dimensions of about twelve feet by twenty feet.

One morning down the canyon from the north came a hurricane force wind. It tipped one house trailer over on the metal horse corral and just rolled the second one over several times until nothing was left of it but some crumbled metal and boards.

**SOME TREES BREAK OFF IN THE MIDDLE.**

**AFTER A BIG WIND IN THE MOUNTAINS**

The trailer that just tipped over had several cases of bottled fruits and vegetables in it that Joy had just canned for the fall hunting season. The broken jars were actually imbedded in the walls and ceiling along with the sticky fruits and vegetables.

Luckily no one was in the trailers at this time or serious injury or death would have been the result. The two canvas tents that sat right at the edge of the area were not damaged at all!

We have a 5,000 gallon water tank that sits upright. It is about ten foot across and fifteen foot high. We installed it on a pad about fifty feet above our subdivision and tree farm. It had a dual purpose of water for the subdivision lots and to furnish water to an irrigation drip system for several thousand small Blue Spruce trees.

I planted large Golden Willow trees on the east and west sides but the north side was only about twenty feet from the mountain. We kept the tank full of water during the summer but had to drain it when cold weather arrived because it was not insulated.

The tank had been in place about three years when another Zephyr, mild breeze, hurricane or whatever the name, came down the mountain side and rolled the tato the bottom of the hill!

**WANT EXCITEMENT? GET CAUGHT IN AN AREA WHERE THIS IS HAPPENING!**

## Wind in the Mountains

Wind in the mountains after forest fires will be hard to imagine for someone that hasn't been there to witness the devastation or imagine the danger involved in being caught in a windstorm. There is nowhere to go to seek safety for you and your clients or horses and mules.

I have lost a couple of friends through the years from falling trees. The trees are very heavy and unforgiving. Prior to the Forest Service "Let it burn policy," forest fires were managed with some semblance of logic. Fires were put out with the burn perimeters restricted to a few miles at most. When a windstorm came up, the green trees in between the fire areas slowed the winds and kept them from becoming hurricane force.

With the dry cycle over the past 20 years or so there are burnt areas stretching from twenty to forty miles wide with no or very few green trees to slow the winds down. In forty plus years I had never even seen snow drifts on the ridge tops but after the fires we had to pack snow shovels to get over several ridges between our camps and the Salmon River.

## Puckerville Situations

For the first couple of years after a forest fire the trees are still able to withstand major windstorms with only a few being blown over each storm. Then as the trees are weakened from decay and rotting conditions it can and does become a nightmare. I will relate a few of my more scary situations.

**RICHARD AND VICKY NELSON AND DAVID WRAY AT CAMP A COUPLE DAYS BEFORE THE BIG WIND / OUTRUN THE FOREST FIRE EXCITEMENT.**

The first one I remember distinctly involved me primarily but also one of my hunters, Richard Nelsen and later that day his wife Vicki and hunting partner Dave Wray as well as my wife Joy.

We were camped at what we called the Twin Creeks Camp at about 7,000 feet near the head of the North Fork of Stoddard Creek.

Richard and I had hunted afoot south from camp to a ridge that separates the North Fork of Stoddard from Stoddard Creek itself.

There were lots of elk tracks and I decided to drop down into the Stoddard drainage a couple thousand feet and then come back up a canyon where I had positioned Richard. My plan was to hopefully push some elk over the ridge top and within shooting range of Richard.

I had just started back up the canyon when the wind came up to gale force or higher. Now imagine if you can, dead fir and ponderosa trees two or three feet in diameter up to one hundred feet high weighing many tons each and scattered every thirty or forty feet in all directions. Imagine the ash, dust, limbs and bark filling the air so you can't see anything except a glimpse now and then between the worst gusts.

Also, the trees break off from ground level to forty or fifty feet up. When the trees break with a big CRACK! there is a few seconds delay before you can see the direction the tree is falling. This is assuming that you can actually see anything. Either way it doesn't leave you much time to run in the right direction.

I was trapped; there was no direction to go to escape the events as they unfolded. I slowly worked my way up the mountain over the next couple of hours between the most violent gusts. There was no time that trees were not falling and cracking on the hillside, sometimes so close that tree tips and limbs would hit right by me. Between gusts I would hurry to get behind the nearest standing tree that I could make out in the dust and ashes.

The wind was primarily down the mountain so the majority of falling trees were coming toward me. However, some would hit other trees and break them off and they might go in other directions.

By the time I reached the ridge top I had watched at least three of the trees that I had stood behind for a little shelter blow down behind me!

On top of the ridge was a small opening about 100 yards across and I stood out in the middle of it until the wind subsided. I was actually throwing up from fear; I kept hollering and whistling for Richard but could not get an answer. I was afraid he had been hurt by some of the falling trees. We had not discussed what to do under those circumstances.

As I worked my way down the main ridge looking for Richard I looked across the canyon and could not believe my eyes! Another forest fire had broken out and was now racing up the mountain towards the only trail for us to get out of there.

I hurried back to camp and found Richard had returned and was o.k. However, we were all now behind the fire and needed to get out of there if we could.

In previous years and previous fires, I had witnessed the fires go from where this one started to the banks of the Salmon River in only a few hours. This is a distance of about eight air miles and the direction we had to go.

Everyone gathered their gear while I wrangled and saddled the stock and we loaded up and headed out.

It takes two or three hours to get to the area where the fire was going up Grassy. We could hear helicopters and watched a few smoke jumpers descend towards the edge of the fire. It was burning over the trail in a few spots but we were able to get through.

On top, the helicopters were landing and dropping men and gear right where the trail goes over. As Joy was coming by one of the forest service guys tossed a big canvas cover off the pile right beside Joy's horse, Hub. Hub jumped nearly out from under her. Needless to say she gave that boy a severe talking-to.

You may ask, "But how come they were trying to put a fire out in the wilderness with the let it burn policy?" Also, it had already burned that same area several times in the past ten years. Who knows? They have tried to explain their fire management policy to me several times. But to the best of my knowledge it hinges on the decision made by whoever is in charge at the moment.

One day about a year after our harrowing day of the wind and forest fire I was across Stoddard Creek with two hunters Frank Shera and Mike Keating from Indiana.

We had the horses tied up and were glassing for elk when another Big Wind came up. Once again, we had nowhere to hide, but this time we were in a forest of smaller trees. There would be literally hundreds of trees going down at once.

We watched a tree break off across the canyon in the same gulch where I had all the excitement the previous year. It hit another and they just kept falling until thirteen trees had cracked and disintegrated after being struck by the first one. It was like a strike in bowling.

In 2002 I had taken my horse Joe and my mule Josie with a little camp and went up in the Nolan Lookout area to look for bighorn rams for a few days. Sheep season would open in about one week and I wanted to have some idea which direction to go to start the hunt.

I descended one of the finger ridges in Kitchen Creek and tied Joe and Josie to trees while I went exploring for rams.

I had dropped down about a mile in distance and several hundred feet in elevation when I heard the crack-clack of horns of fighting bighorn rams. The sounds come from up the canyon near where I had tied the horse and mule. I headed back towards the sounds of the fighting rams when from nowhere up came another huge wind with the trees cracking all around me.

I knew of an opening with no trees back up the ridge from my horse and mule. I hustled to get back to them and get them up there to safety if possible, assuming they were still o.k. I got to them, they were all right, and we made it up to the center of the opening and away from falling trees.

It was nearly dark and I let Joe and Josie graze in the opening where we were safe. It is a long night with wind howling like banshees and trees cracking close by all night long.

## A Very Close One!

I had sold my outfitting business and had been helping the buyer get established when another big wind filled the trail with down trees.

Chris Smith and I were cutting logs out of the trail with a couple of cross cut saws. Chris and his wife, Dwina Noesbar, own a river outfitting business called Kook-A-Burra Expeditions.

It was a perfectly calm day with not a breath of air. I was kneeling down sawing a low tree across the trail when I heard a tree break off. Chris was sawing a tree just behind me. I looked up and a lodge pole about 8" through was falling directly toward me and only a partial second from cracking me on the head. Somehow I instinctively moved my head and pivoted my shoulders out of the way as the tree crashed within inches! How I moved that quick I'm not sure.

I had tried to be a boxer in my younger years and feel that instinctively dodging, or at least trying to dodge punches had probably saved my life on this occasion.

I turned around and looked at Chris. He was ok, but we were both weak from the near miss.

The next day we recruited hunters Mike Keating and Frank Shera, once again, to help saw trees so we could get to Stoddard Lookout and try to find some elk.

It took three more full days to get enough trees out of the trail to get there, a distance of only two miles! Once while we were resting I told them "Look at the bright side!" It is only costing you $600.00 a day for the experience and privilege of sawing trees with a "Misery whip"!

During that hunt alone, we cut over three hundred trees of various sizes just to get the horses and mules along trails to do a little hunting!

**You may get the impression that I am not the greatest fan of wilderness management and you would be correct.**

# Chapter 6

# Alaska Sheep Hunt – Ptarmigan Lake

One year Bill Kornell, Ken Smith and I had flown my Cessna 206, 8647Z to Alaska on a hunting trip.

We landed on the Alaska Highway near the Yukon border and tied the plane down at a landmark roadhouse, motel, bar and café called Matt's Place. It had a couple of what I would call "Claims to Fame".

First claim; Matt had left Anchorage in the 1920's because it was getting too crowded with people and hiked cross country for several weeks to a place that he assumed would give him the lifetime of solitude he desired.

Guess What? They built the Alaska Highway within a few hundred feet of his cabin door. (Murphy's Law and The Matt Factor)!

He figured if you can't beat them join them. He constructed the facilities to cater to construction crews and road traffic with an occasional bit of air traffic thrown in.

Second claim; he built a "Three hole" outhouse for the convenience of traveling families. It is the only one I have ever seen.

While we were there, three friends of mine from Austin, Minnesota, Stan Christensen, Len Harber, and Brian Harber, arrived to hunt at Ptarmigan Lake with Outfitter Urban Rahoi.

When they headed home they left a calendar from Stan's electrical company with Matt to give to me. Somehow, in the chaos of us leaving, Matt forgot to give it to me so he mailed it. The postage was $3.00.

I kept thinking I would get back there and pay him but several years went by without this happening.

A friend of mine from Hailey, Robert Swaner was going to Alaska so I gave him $3.00 to pay Matt when he went by. It had taken me a long time and a round about way to pay my debt but I finally got it done.

We had been hunting for a few days west of the lake, Bill and Ken decided to go back and hunt to the east toward the Yukon border.

There was a big mountain range that ran east and west and ended up back close to the lake. I figured it would be a nice two or three day hunt in great looking game country.

Bill and Ken left one morning to head back to the lake and I strapped on my pack frame and hiked about a half mile to the toe of the mountain I would be climbing.

I had nearly made it to the ridge I was going to start up when I saw two grizzly bears coming down toward me. My first thought was "I don't need another set-to with grizzly bears." (See the Grizzly Charge), page 159 of "The Potts Factor Versus Murphy's Law.") That incident had the result of my luckily being able to kill the grizzly about

**8647ZULU TIED DOWN AT MATTS PLACE ON THE ALASKA HIWAY JUST INSIDE THE ALASKA/YUKON BORDER**

one jump before he hit me.

I lifted my pack frame off, got my rifle, loaded one in the barrel and put my binoculars to my eyes to get a better look at the bears.

Guess what? The bears had shrunk and dissolved into a pair of porcupines! I didn't even know there were porcupines in Alaska and I guess I was just a little over excitable after my previous bear encounter.

I walked on past my "porky bears" and commenced the climb of probably three or four thousand feet to the crest of the mountain. I was a few hundred feet from the top when I looked around the hillside and saw six dall rams bedded on the hillside.

## Ram Interaction

One of the rams was pretty good sized and I decided to try and get closer after they had moved to somewhere out of sight. They were farther away then I felt comfortable taking the shot.

After a few hours the rams all stood up at the same time and looked in the same direction up the mountain. Over the top and coming down directly toward the other six rams were ten more rams with another big ram in this bunch.

I will try to explain the unique interaction between the rams. The larger ram of the herd of ten was the last one. As the smaller rams in this bunch arrived at the six ram herd each ram would go over to the big ram of the six. They would each rub their horns on his neck and shoulders and then go on by. He would appear to completely ignore them as this scenario was playing out.

As the big ram from the group of ten got closer I assumed I would be watching one hell of a ram fight when he arrived. What happened was the farthest thing from my mind.

The big ram with the 10 herd walked directly toward six big ram and paused within about three feet. Neither ram appeared to even know the other ram was on this planet.

**TYPICAL SHEEP HUNTER BEDGROUND!**

It reminded me of two bullies on the playground ignoring each other until the time was right for one to make his move. By the time this had all played out the smaller rams from both bunches had descended the mountain for a few hundred yards and were now in sight again.

As the big rams followed out of sight I still couldn't make a stalk on them because of all the sheep in sight below me.

It was nearly dark by then so I decided to camp (as in lay out my pad, sleeping bag and bag cover) and try them the next day.

Guess what? It snowed about six inches and was fogged in the next day. I never saw the rams again.

I descended to a glacial spring of icy slush-filled water and found out you could build an edible gruel of Mountain House dehydrated beef stew, dissolved somewhat, in icy slush!

**THE FIRST 6 RAMS**

**PART OF THE RAM HERD AFTER THEY ALL GOT TOGETHER.**

# Chapter 7

# Joy & Ken Johnson's B. C. Stone Sheep Hunt

Our long time friend from Los Altos, California had been in treatment for leukemia for about eighteen months. (See Ken Johnson and the Rocket Mule,) page 94 of "Look Down on the Stars"). Ken liked to hunt, and he and his brother Marvin had taken a bighorn ram in Idaho.

Ken was taking chemotherapy and would try to get the treatments scheduled and distanced so he would be able to arrange a couple weeks each fall to hunt. He and Joy and I had gone to Alaska the previous year. And we had each gotten dall rams. We had booked a stone ram hunt for Ken and Joy with me going along as a non-hunter but to help them as much as I could.

The hunt left a lot to be desired from many standpoints but did have some interesting high-lights. On our trip by pack string into the area we were going to look for stone rams, our route followed up the Toad River and we traveled along on an old Indian trapping trail.

The Indian camp was on a small lake that appeared to be near the mouth of the Toad River and consisted of a few small cabins. The guide told us the Indian trapper had learned to read and write by studying the lettering on canned food labels.

Every half mile or so along the old trail would be a tree that would have a side flattened with an axe. The smooth spot would usually be about a foot to a foot and half wide and from one foot to three feet long. The flat places were similar to the flat sides of a 2"x12" board and served as a type of diary.

On each flat sided tree would be a short sentence or two recording the day's happenings as the trapper passed by. A typical sentence would start something like "Dec. 11, 1927, snow 37 inches, temperature 17° below, caught Lynx cat here today". The next trip would be penciled directly underneath so there may be several years of happenings documented on each tree.

The flat sides on the trees were usually about eight feet high, just right to read from the back of a horse. I assumed the winter's snow would usually be three feet deep or so and the trapper would be on

**JOY POTTS AND DALL RAM FROM PRIOR ALASKA HUNT**

snowshoes or skies. After several miles we could hardly wait to read the next diary.

We passed by a small log cabin in good repair, at the edge of a small swampy clearing. Standing upright against the cabin wall were several wooden wolf and lynx stretchers for drying the hides. We asked the guide if the cabin was still used and his reply was, "No, the modern Indians keep it all in good repair for the trappers eventual return from the happy hunting grounds".

When we arrived at another cabin that was the outfitters hunting camp it was in total disarray. A grizzly or grizzlies had broken in and also got in their cache twenty feet in the air and eaten or ruined all their supplies.

Not much food had been brought with us so the next few days we were badly short of rations. They had brought a case of Spam so that was basically it. The outfitters dad was the cook and after a few days he asked Joy to cook as he had exhausted all his recipes for cooking Spam!

One morning we spotted a good stone ram walking around the mountain above camp. The guide, Joy and I headed up to try for him. About half way up we passed by a fresh grizzly kill of a caribou. When we finally found the ram he was in the cliffs directly below us about 80 yards straight down. That's when we found he only had one horn! It was a beautiful horn about 39" or 40"long. We talked it over and Joy decided she would wait for one with two horns. If we had known that would be her only chance at a legal ram we might have not passed on him.

**KEN JOHNSON AND STAN POTTS ON PREVIOUS ALASKA HUNT AT PTARMIGAN LAKE.**

On the way back we put Joy on a game trail that went by the cabin and the guide and I went scouting further around the mountain. When he and I returned back to the cabin - NO JOY! The guide headed back up to where we had left her. I went after horses as I didn't figure I could make it back up the hill for lack of energy. I had already used my day's supply. I caught the horses and headed up. I met them part way, "WHEW", Joy had got on a different trail and had spent a couple hours getting it unraveled.

We all (especially Joy) heaved a sigh of relief because of the recent grizzly kill nearby.

It was raining everyday and Joy and I and the guide spent three days in a tent made for two people trying to keep somewhat dry.

We had gone to a high basin that was their hotspot. The rain had slackened so we could see as we walked up on two rams, but the guide said they were too borderline legal (not quite full curl) to chance shooting. We saw one other ram but the guide wouldn't try a stalk because he didn't think we could get there.

With all the rain and Ken and his guide not seeing anything, Ken decided to have his guide take him out so he could fly home. It was definitely not a fun hunt for Ken in his weakened condition. It would be his last hunt.

The last day of Joy's hunt was fogged in all day so no chance for a ram for Joy. We had spotted 12 rams the night before about three miles away that had at least five legal rams in the bunch. That is a real letdown when you find them just as the hunt comes to an end.

# Chapter 8

## The Slender Cord

About 1980 I received a call from Dr. Charles Guess, of Moscow, Idaho. He had received an alternate tag on the Middle Fork of the Salmon River for a bighorn ram and wondered if I could take him on the hunt. I called Con Hourihan at the Taylor Ranch to see if he could pack us to the area. We would then hunt on foot from there. Con said he would be able to pack us in, so Dr. Guess and I worked out the details for an early September hunt.

I flew into the Taylor Ranch in our Cessna 180; 9175G to meet Dr. Guess and Con Hourihan's pack string. It would take us about five hours to get to the area where I wanted to start the hunt. After we were dropped off near a small spring that would be our main camp, Dr. Guess and I were able to visit and learn a little about each other.

Dr. Guess had just returned from a cape buffalo hunt in Africa. He told me that the previous year he had been involved in a nearly fatal goring by an enraged cape buffalo. The bull ran a horn up through his groin and into his intestines. Then beat him against trees and brush, Doc passed out from the pain and when he came too he said his vision showed many upright black tubes wobbling around with lots of chanting and singing.

He was on a cot in a native hut and all the tribesmen were dancing around the cot he was laying on. He was looking at the dancers legs.

When Doc came to enough to survey his damage he knew it was very serious. His intestines had been opened up with major trauma and he knew the probability of peritonitis and infection imminent. Soon thereafter a doctor arrived to give him shots and what care was possible at these primitive surroundings. He was then taken to a hospital for treatment and somehow serious infection and peritonitis were adverted.

Doctor Guess said he felt he must return to find out if the mental trauma of the goring could be over come. He was able to do so and killed a trophy cape buffalo bull.

The next morning after only a few hours of glassing I found a band of rams. Our attempted stalk "severiously" spooked them out of the canyon they had been living in. If I had known how tough the hunt would become I guarantee you I would have taken more time and tried much harder to have made the first stalk successful.

We packed up our pack frames for a three or four day trip and headed out in the direction the rams had headed.

The next afternoon I located either that herd or another nice band of rams. They were located a couple thousand feet below us. We carefully maneuvered into shooting range and waited for the rams to get up to feed so we could pick one out for the shot.

The rams got up to feed, we picked the one we wanted and the results were not good. Doc missed him several times.

We knew the rifle was zeroed in when we started so I attributed the missing to the dreaded "Ram Fever" that has plagued hunters in all parts of the world.

We had made our stalk down thru some very bad cliffs and had left our big pack frames up at the top of them. It was now getting dark and I decided we would have to wait for daylight to find our way back up. We had drank what water we had taken with us, so we were now very dry.

I explained the situation to Dr. Guess; he said he would like to get back to our pack frames. I told him I would also, but there was only one possible way up through the cliffs and it would take some light to locate it.

He then said, "But I have to get back to my pack frame, my nitroglycerine pills are in it!"

I then came somewhat unglued, "Why didn't you tell me you had a bad heart"?

"I figured if you knew that you wouldn't take me to the good places".

I guess I could see his logic but that didn't solve our problem.

At the base of the cliff where we are sitting in the dark we could hear running water that sounded pretty close. It sounded just around the cliff and down. When you are very thirsty the agonizing gurgle of nearby water makes you try strange things.

I pack 100 feet of ¼ nylon rope in my fanny pack along with lunch, canteen, fire starter etc. I tied one end to a nearby tree, took our two empty canteens and went over the edge with my flashlight to try and locate the deliriously beautiful gurgling water.

My adventure proved unsuccessful. I arrived back to Doc with the bad news and we continued to discuss our predicament. You might keep in mind that this nylon rope would play a couple more important parts to this saga.

I noticed that the moon was slowly casting a little more light onto the cliffs. I decided that if I could definitely find the route we had descended that we would be able to go back up. It was not a long way, probably two or three hundred yards to extra water and his nitro pills, plus some food and our sleeping bags.

As the moon cast more light I was finally able to locate the chute we had come down and we were able to get to our packs about midnight. After sleeping till daylight we found the water source, replenished our water and went back to try and locate rams.

The following day we spotted either one of the previous ram bunches or a new group. No matter, there were some very nice ones.

I decided that with Doc not being able to place his shots where we needed them that somehow we would have to try to get closer, hopefully under 100 yards.

These rams were lying on a bluff only a few hundred feet above the river and with trees and undulating terrain. That appeared to give us greater possibility for a chance at a close shot. We kept the main pack frames with us until we were within a couple hundred yards. We then dropped them and eased on still closer. When we were about 100 yards I asked Doc if this would work. He said he would like to try to get a little closer.

The rams were lying down in a straight line facing away from us. I told him to ease down to where he felt comfortable, get a solid rest and kill the right hand ram. Doc got down to a flat rock about three feet high and placed the gun on the solid rest, about 80 yards from the rams. After what seemed like an unnaturally long time he fired. All the rams jumped to their feet and raced around the bluff to the right.

Doc took off at a full bore run as if to try and intercept them, I couldn't believe it! Now a cinch shot wasted. I went back up and got both pack frames and descended to the spot the rams had been laying. There about a foot under the targeted rams' hip was a hole blown in the dirt. Around it were bullet fragments, a few sheep hairs and a couple drops of blood. I had been focused on the ram and when he had jumped up it seemed as if he had straightened his left hind leg somewhat unnaturally.

As I was mulling over what to do in my mind I heard a gunshot in the direction of rams and hunter travel and at least a half mile away.

I followed the running ram tracks and in a few minutes here come Doc running back toward me. He was stripped down to his T-shirt and sweating profusely. When we got to one another, he gasped, "I need some help! I shot the ram and he fell over the bluff!"

The bluff was several hundred feet down. I had about come to the end of all possible patience! As I started to light into him about all the lashups he broke into a grin.

"No, I have the ram. But I do need some help!"

When we arrived at the beautiful ram he was about two feet from the edge and tethered to a tree with Doc's rifle sling and belt to keep him from falling over the bluff. Doc knew I had about run out of forbearance and he figured his method of alleviating the tension would work. It did! We found that the bullet had blown up in the ground and a portion of the bullet had exploded upward just puncturing the skin on the rams hind leg! I guess the ram thought he was hurt for as he followed the other rams around the cliff he turned on his back trail that Doc was following him on. Bad mistake for the ram as Doc was close enough this time to make the shot count.

Now, to try to get the ram meat, cape, horns and ourselves back to our base camp. It turned into another major adventure.

In the course of our travels I had found out that Doc had not

**STAN POTTS WITH DR. GUESS' GREAT RAM. (Note: THE SLENDER CORD KEEPS RAM FROM GOING OVER CLIFF.)**

told me about his heart problem or the need for nitro pills to keep the old ticker functioning. He had also neglected to inform me he was deathly afraid of cliffs and vertical country! We were now facing a bunch of it.

We cleaned and skinned the ram and placed the boned out meat on rocks and mahogany limbs to dry and cool out. We took some of the meat from the rib cage and after it had cooled we built a mahogany wood fire and barbecued our supper. It was a far better meal than Mountain House! ©

**DR CHARLES GUESS AND HIS FINE IDAHO BIGHORN.**

After a good nights rest we packed up and headed around the top of the bluff looking for a way down to the river. After going all the way back past where the rams had been when he first shot, I did not find a way down so I left Doc and the packs and retraced on past where he had killed the ram. Still unable to find a decent way completely off the bluff. I figured the best possibility I could find was definitely not what I knew Doc was anticipating.

He would have to descend on the little ¼" nylon cord! The rope supposedly had a breaking strength of 250 pounds new so I knew we had some cushion. My problem was convincing Doc that it was our only way short of back the way we had come with a climb of around 4,000 ft with heavily loaded pack frames.

We got to the spot I had picked and tied the rope to a mahogany tree and dropped it over the bluff. It appeared to have about twenty feet of rope left so we had a descent of approximately seventy five to eighty feet. I told Doc I would go down first and figure out the system so I could explain how to do it to him. Then he could lower each pack frame of eighty to one hundred pounds. Then I could untie them and Doc would come down last. I had never attempted this before so there were major experiments involved.

My first mistake: I decided that with no knots in the rope, which I knew would weaken it, I would take a single wrap around one hand, go down a couple of feet, grip with the other hand and then slide the unwrapped hand down and repeat the process until I got to the bottom. Good plan or what? Or what butted in.

I made my wrap around the right hand which would be the upper hand. You probably already see the folly. When you get down two feet the upper hand with the wrap is tight and you can't slide it down the rope. Back up I went and I put wraps on lower hand and sure enough it was working.

Somewhere I had picked up on the fact that you place your feet against the cliff face – lean out backward and just basically walk down backwards. It worked great, well probably not great but at least satisfactorily.

I told Doc to watch me and after I had the system figured out I would re-explain it to him for his descent. It would be hard to explain or even draw the look in, or the size of, Doc's eyeballs as I was going down. I made it, had Doc pull the rope up and lower the pack frames one by one. So far so good, now for the critical test, seeing if all this could overpower Doc's fear of heights and the cliffs (trepidation or terror would not explain it).

I re-explained the system, wrap around the lower hand, lean backward and ease downward to the bottom. Everything worked great for about two steps down the cliff then I think Doc looked down between his feet, panicked and clutched the rope to his chest. He spun around with his back to the cliff and his legs out into the air and there we were! This would probably be the time to insert the caption, "Continued Next Month!"

Unfortunately this was a real life drama unfolding and something had to be done quickly or there would be a mountain tragedy in the next few minutes.

Now Doc is a big man probably 6'2 and 230 or so pounds. I am 220 or so, now remember the breaking strength of the new ¼" rope is around 250 and the rope is not new at this point in time.

I had no choice except what I did. I went up the rope, turned Doc around so he could get his feet back against the cliff. I put my hands under his on the rope, placed my feet against the cliff so that he would step just above mine. I told him to move ever so gently and we slowly and carefully came down the rope to the bank of the river.

We had been suspended over fifty feet in the air on a slender cord theoretically capable of supporting only approximately one-half the weight it was subjected to. Good luck for sure when we badly needed it!

We rested and regrouped after our ordeal. Then we loaded up and walked up the bank of the river. It was only about an hour till dark and I knew we had one more bad cliff to get around. And now we will have no rope. It is tied to the tree at the top of the cliff.

After about a mile and just as we were coming upon the bad cliff we had to get around, I looked up the river and on the other side was a rubber boat and a hundred yards or so up on a bench of ground was a bonfire. I hollered and two guys walked out and looked over at us. They came down and got in their boat and rowed over to us. I planned on asking them if I could hire them to get the boat up above the next cliff and then get us back on our side of the river.

When they got to us I recognized two friends of mine. Jerry Meyers who was at the time in the Real Estate business and had also helped me on several hunting trips for mountain lion. He had a sheep tag also and was looking for a ram. With him was Gary Powers, a conservation officer from Salmon, who had taken a few days off to help Jerry with his search for a ram. I asked them for their help and we crossed the river and then packed the boat through the brush for a few hundred yards above some small rapids and they got us back to our side of the river.

Our base camp was just above us a few hundred yards. Gary said, "I guess, as long as we're here, I might just as well look at your license and tag."

**STAN POTTS AND JERRY MEYERS WITH GARY POWERS IN BOAT HELPING WITH OUR MUCH APPRECIATED RIVER CROSSING.**

Guess what, they were in Doc's duffle bag and we could have been in serious trouble. I offered to run up and get them but Gary said, "No, I know you have the tag".

The next day I walked to the Taylor Ranch about nine miles to make arrangements to have Con's packer come get our camp, sheep and gear.

Doc gave me the meat from the ram. I flew to Hailey and he flew to Challis and then drove to Salmon to have his ram horns plugged and checked at the regional office of the Idaho Department of Fish and Game.

I was cutting up the ram meat in my kitchen when Lee Frost, the local conservation officer, and another officer drove into the yard and then walked to the door.

Lee said, "Stan did you just come out of the Middle Fork with a sheep hunter"?

I replied "Yes".

Lee said, "He is at the Salmon office and his tag is not for that area"!

"WHAT NEXT COULD HAPPEN"?! My heart sank. Would the problems never end?

Lee used my telephone and after about an hour of calls back and forth to the State Office in Boise and the Salmon office the mystery was finally solved.

Somehow, with Doc's tag being an alternate tag, the computer had put out two tags with identical numbers except one of them was for a California Big Horn in Owyhee County. This was in the early days in the use of computers. Some times they still don't work correctly.

That brings us to the conclusion of a ram hunt that resulted in a great ram but that could have definitely transpired a little more simply. I guess if it had been too simple this story would never have been penned. After over one hundred ram hunts from Nevada to the Yukon, and outfitting and guiding clients to seventy six bighorn rams it seems that the hunts that went correctly and simply just don't make the story cut!

## Chapter 9

# Billy Havens' 2002 Auction Tag Hunt

Idaho is one of many states that issue a couple of sheep tags each year to raise dollars for the conservation and enhancement of Bighorn sheep. Many other species also benefit but the dollars raised from the Idaho Bighorn sheep auction tag and the Idaho Lottery tag are primarily earmarked for the sheep programs.

I was actively involved in the lobbying and testifying before the Legislature. With much appreciated support from Senator Ron Beitelspacher and Pam Ahrens we were able to finally get both of these tags to become a reality. Not many people are aware of it but I actually wrote the bill for the lottery tag on a Red Lion Hotel napkin at the winter Idaho Outfitters and Guides Convention. With the support and help of the Idaho Chapter of the Foundation for North American Wild Sheep the bill passed the legislature with the nearly identical wording as on my Red Lion napkin.

As a longtime outfitter specializing in Bighorn sheep hunts I was able to outfit and guide several of the auction and lottery tag holders though out the years. The most recent hunt was 2002 Auction tag holder, Billy Havens from New Mexico.

We started his hunt near my home at Colson Creek on the Salmon River but after a few days of trying to battle road closures, trail closures and forest fires, we gave up and went to the north end of the Lost River Range, east of Challis, Idaho.

About the third day we were hunting a canyon that runs to the north into the Pahsimeroi Valley. We were looking for a big ram that Judd Whitworths' friend had seen a couple days before. Out in the flat we saw a band of Judds' domestic sheep near the mouth of the canyon.

We passed a pickup parked out in the sagebrush. We didn't give it any thought until a couple of hours later when a fusillade of rifle shots commenced behind us and down the canyon.

There were at least three different calibers involved and it was a weird situation for the next two or three hours.

Billy Havens the hunter, and Holton Quinn and I were the ones in the canyon. Every few minutes there would be from a dozen to thirty or forty shots fired. Not like shooting at anything but more like the shooters were trying to see how fast and how many shots they could fire in the shortest period of time. Any chance of finding the big ram vanished with the first volley of shots.

Now we are trying to stay under cover (as in behind trees), and ascertain what is really happening. Are the shots meant to drive us away because of someone's jealousy of Billy's ability to purchase the tag at a price several times the average yearly wage in the area? Were the shots meant to harass the herder of Judd's sheep? Were they actually watching the big ram and shooting around him to chase him off?

It's one of life's little mysteries because we never actually saw anyone. The total amount of shots fired over two or three hours was several hundred to a few thousand. I don't know how possibly only three or four people were able to pack that amount of weight in bullets alone. The pickup was still out in the sage brush when we left and other than telling our story we never tried any harder to unravel the events.

The next day we hunted a new area and Holton found three rams for us. One of them was really nice and I tried to get Billy within shooting range in a blizzard. Didn't work! Another one of Potts's Famous Blown Stalks!

I then contacted Doug Sayer of Premier Outfitters and hired him and two of his guides to help us on the hunt. They had been keeping track of some good rams in the hopes of one of the tag holders hiring them so it worked out good for all of us.

We met Doug at Amy Lou's Steakhouse in Mackay for breakfast the next morning. His guides, Jim Warner and Will Marcroft, had left at about 3:00 am to try to locate the rams and we would hike up the mountain behind them.

Billy's friend, Greg Price, had driven up from New Mexico and would be doing a video of the remainder of the hunt. After daylight we headed up the mountain in the direction Jim and Will had gone and after a couple of hours were met by Jim. He informed us that they had three nice rams located but that the rams were not together and would be hard to stalk. They were about 400 yards apart. Trying to stay out of sight of all three while working into shooting range of the best one would take lots of skill not to mention a fair share of good luck.

The rams were in the open shale hillsides well above the last timber and brush that could be used for cover.

Will Marcroft took Billy around the mountain in the trees to get closer to the best two rams. The rest of us would stay behind to signal them if the rams did any major moving while the hunter and guide were in the trees and couldn't see the rams. Two of the three rams were shooters. We estimated them both to be very near the Boone & Crockett minimum score of 180 points.

Just before dark Will and Billy were able to get within long shooting range and Billy was able to kill one of the two best rams.

The ram had a green score of around 178 points so our estimates were very close and Billy collected a fine Idaho bighorn.

**GUIDE WILL MARCROFT, HUNTER BILLY HAVENS AND OUTFITTER DOUG SAYER WITH BILLYS' FINE LOST RIVER RAM**

# Chapter 10

# Yukon Sheep Hunt With Near Catastrophe

Joy, I, and our good friend Dick Hall flew our Cessna 180, 2242C, to Dawson City, Yukon in 1973 to hunt with outfitter Stan Reynolds and his wife Ruth.

Stan met us in Dawson City and loaded our friends Jess and Dorothy Taylor from the Taylor Ranch and Dr. Cliff Johnson from Boise into Stan's Cessna 180. They had flown up commercially. We followed him northwest about 150 miles to his TNT mountain camp.

Stan had carved a nice landing strip out of the trees and willows along the bank of the Tatonduk River and had constructed several cabins including a school house for his children. Mom Ruth was the school teacher.

Joy and I along with Stan Reynolds took a little packstring up the Tatonduk River a few miles and then branched off up a smaller drainage and camped for a few days. I was successful in killing my Dall ram that would be the third leg of my hoped for Grand Slam. I also got a nice grizzly plus a 55" Yukon Moose.

Dr. Johnson killed a dall ram, a grizzly bear and a wolverine, but Jess Taylor was unable to get his much sought after mountain grizzly. They hunted in a different direction with two guides.

It rained nearly every day on our little campout and the canyon bottom was nearly a lake when we headed back down toward the base camp at TNT Mountain. I knew that you should never admit you know anything about horses when you show up in an outfitter's camp. However, I was sort of trapped as Stan knew I was an outfitter and if I didn't know anything about horses I at least should! Consequently and correspondingly, I was issued a big four year old mare that was in the initial stages of training as in, she had been ridden SEVERAL times.

I long ago found out the meaning of the word several. Two or more! The American Heritage Dictionary, second college edition: 1) being of a number more than two or three but not many!

Anyway, she was a big sweetheart and I hopefully helped her along in the training process. There are no horse trails as such, and travel consists of following moose and bear trails through the brush as best you can. Because of no trails, horses are not pigtailed and strung together as we usually do here in the states. They are each belled and fitted with a muzzle of heavy mesh screen. That allows the pack animals to drink but not eat while traveling. The system is to remove the muzzle at night so they can eat and the bells are on each one so you have some idea where they are. Most of the time it is so brushy that you can usually only see a few of the pack horses at one time.

During travel one rider that knows where he is going (and hopefully how to get there), takes the lead. In this case it was Stan

**WE FLY UP THE YUKON RIVER UNDER THE FOG AND ALONGSIDE STAN REYNOLDS' CESSNA 180.**

Reynolds. The last riders, Joy and I, follow along and hopefully keep the stragglers all headed in the general direction taken by the leader.

We were traveling along with no problems except riding in a foot or two of water with no trail. I heard Stan holler up ahead of me, I speeded the big mare up as much as I could and by Stan hollering got to where he and his horse were nearly submerged in the water.

A big tree had blown over and a root ball had left a four or five foot hole in the ground. Stan's horse had fallen into it and couldn't get his footing to get out.

In the fall he had pinned Stan's leg against the dirt and roots so that Stan couldn't get away from the horse and out of the hole full of water. When the horse would lunge it would just mash Stan harder against the hole. Remember, they are in four or five feet of water with no way to see or tell what is going on below Stan's and the horses head and shoulders.

I moved my big mare up as close as I could and placed the loop of my lariat rope around his saddle horn and took a couple of dallies around the saddle horn on My Big Pet Mare. I was able to take the

**THE RIVER CROSSING THAT TOOK JOY'S HORSE ALONG WITH THE CURRENT.**

horse weight off of Stan's leg enough for him to scramble out.

Stan wasn't seriously hurt and we were then able to pull his horse out of the hole. It was still scary as there was no way of telling if the horse's legs were tangled in roots and would break as I pulled with the big mare. Other than a bruised outfitter and his horse we all lucked out of a very tense and possibly fatal incident that turned into just another mountain story.

Other than some exciting river crossings, one of which took Joy's horse (and Joy of course!) along with the current, we made it back to the lodge OK.

One evening after supper I took Stan & Ruth's children with me and we walked down toward the river for a mile or so. (Dan, if you read this you might remember.) I had a predator call I had made out of the tip of a cow horn and wanted to see if it would work to call in wolves.

The kids were from about five to ten years old. We all sat down on the ground around a big willow bush and I blew loudly on my "Yipper" call. Immediately there was a great crashing of willows coming our way. All of a sudden where there had been several feet between the kids and I now there were four little backs backed up to mine. And we were probably within a four foot circle!

About then through the brush came a very angry cow moose that appeared very intent on stomping a wolf to death. Luckily she decided we were harmless and went on her way.

**STAN REYNOLDS' DAUGHTER BRUSHES HER HORSE NEXT TO THE BIG PET MARE.**

# *Chapter 11*

# Earl Lunceford's Idaho Bighorn Hunt - With Engaging Highlights, Including How I Met Elmer Earl

In 1993 Earl Lunceford from Coeur d'Alene, Idaho, purchased the Idaho sheep auction tag. The tag is valid in all the Idaho sheep areas.

Earl wanted to see if he could get an old broomed off ram that might make the record book. We decided to concentrate on a newly opened area on the Snake River south of Lewiston, Idaho.

I had guided Earl on a sheep hunt on the Salmon River a few years prior to this one that had ended unsuccessfully. Forest fires were once again raging all across the Idaho sheep country during our hunt. We had passed on a couple of legal but smaller rams early on this hunt and then spent the entire last afternoon within a couple hundred yards of a bunch of rams with big tracks that were fighting in smoke so thick that we were never able to look at them.

After Earl had bought the tag he called me with the news and basically told me he didn't think I could skunk him twice so hired me to outfit and guide him.

I drove to Lewiston a couple of times during the summer to learn the area and get a feel for what we might have a chance at as far as the type of ram Earl was hoping for. It is a nine hour drive to the sheep area from my house, but the scouting trips showed me that there were some fine rams in the area.

I hired Travis Bullock, a young guide who guided hunting and white water river trips for my neighbors, Steve and Michelle Zettle. They owned our old hunting business at the Taylor Ranch plus float permits on the Middle Fork of the Salmon River. Travis would help on the hunt by looking for rams and running the video camera.

We had located a herd of rams on opening morning but they were a couple of miles across a deep canyon. As we watched them while deciding our best plan of attack, several gun shots erupted and the rams took off at a dead run. With the binoculars we soon picked up two hunters working their way toward where the rams had been. The men then started working on a downed ram.

We followed the departing rams with the spotting scope and decided the best ram was still with the bunch. The ram herd moved a mile or so and then bedded down in some cliffs. We decided to be in that area come daylight the next morning.

We left our camp about 3:00am with flashlights. We had several miles to travel through country that none of us had been in before. Our route and direction proved correct and we located the ram herd soon after we arrived at the cliffs, where they had been the evening before.

Unfortunately the rams were traveling away from us and losing elevation fast. We decided they were descending to a creek for water and our best bet to get a shot was to go down the mountain part way until we found a decent vantage point and then wait until we located the rams coming back up.

We found a good lookout point and waited several hours but could see no rams. Evening was approaching so we reverted to what (in sheep hunting vernacular) is know as alternate plan B, one more of many changed plans.

As we descended toward the creek I looked down and saw ram horns sticking out of a brushy gulch. The rams were bedded down in the shade of the willows. We got out of sight, worked into shooting range and I tied Earls' and my walking sticks together for a shooting rest.

Travis went down below with the video camera and hollered them out of the brush. Earl killed his old broomed off dream ram that officially scored 183⅝ Boone and Crocket points. Earl had his record book ram!

Now our wheels are all on top of the mountain. We are nearly to the bottom and all roads are behind locked gates. I asked Travis to take one load of sheep meat and go to the Snake River and see if he could flag down a boat to take us across the river to the Washington State side. Earl and I would bring the rest of the meat plus the cape and horns and come slowly down behind him.

If we could get across we would be on a road and hopefully, be able to hire someone to take us down to Clarkston, Washington, across

**EARL LUNCEFORD AND HIS RECORD BOOK RAM WE NAMED "ROCKY"**

**STAN POTTS AND "ROCKY"**

to Lewiston and up to our camp and pickups.

In a short time we saw Travis coming back towards us. He reported there was a ranch on the river and the owner would haul us back to the top in his International Scout. That is how we met Captain Elmer Earl, one of the last steam ship captains in the United States.

After a couple of hours of story telling and a couple of cocktails we started our trip up the narrow mountain road that was very slow and very terrifying! The old scout was only running on (possibly) three of the original four cylinders. It was burning oil horribly and smoked like an old coal powered steam locomotive.

With four of us, three pack frames and a big horn ram it would barely travel on the level road. Elmer's system of going up was to take a mighty run at the top until the engine died, then jump on the brakes as we careened backwards down the hill. Remember, on a mountain road one side is dirt and the other side is air!

It was pitch black and about midnight. After a few of these exciting forays Earl got out with his precious ram horns to walk.

He said he didn’t mind getting killed in the wreck he knew would happen the first time we went over the edge backwards, but he didn’t want the sheep horns to be ruined!

Travis and I got out and pushed until we got to a semi-wide spot where we could get Elmer turned around. I gave Elmer $100.00, thanked him, and we packed our pack frames and Earls ram on to the top of the mountain. Took a couple hours more but at least we made it alive!

One of the interesting stories Elmer told us that I can remember was about the Nez Perce Indians. He said they crossed the river by his place twice a year.

Once in the Spring coming from the Washington side to summer in the Camas Prairie area and once in the Fall going back across to the Washington side for winter.

Elmer said they were great horsemen and would camp a day or two along the riverbank just below his house, and that their method of training the wild horses was very unique. They would herd several of the horses including broke and unbroken (trained and untrained), out into the water where it was deep enough that the horses had to swim. Then the younger Indian boys would swim out, grab a wild horse by the mane, crawl aboard and swim on the horse's back for awhile before the older Indians allowed the horse and rider out on the beach.

By then the horse had become somewhat accustomed to the rider and didn’t usually buck as hard or as long. He also said one young Indian boy was much better at it than the other boys (riding the ones that bucked). Elmer found out later the boy's name was Jackson Sundown. Jackson Sundown went on to become one of the early World Champion Saddle Bronc Riders.

For a history of that portion of the Snake River and the early paddlewheel and steamship travel, read “Hells Canyon - A River Trip” by Elmer Earl. It was printed by Lewiston Printing, 145 A Thain, Lewiston, Idaho 83501

**THE COVER FROM CAPTAIN ELMER EARL'S BOOK**

# Chapter 12

# I Wasn't Really Lost (The World Got Turned Around)

Living a goodly portion of your life in the mountains there are situations that occasionally arise where you desire to migrate from point A to point B and somehow point B isn't located where it is suppose to be. I will relate a couple of instances that come to mind regarding same.

They both happened in what is now the Frank Church Wilderness in Central Idaho. About two and a quarter million acres of mountains, canyons, rivers, trees and rocks and not many street signs!

The first turnaround time was on a late November elk and deer hunt. Members of this group were Gerald Twitchell, Jerry Twitchell, Lawrence Halverson and I. Lawrence was the Mormon Bishop and how he got involved with the rest of us heathen types, I'm not sure! Probably could be described as a fateful decision on his part.

We were camped near Coyote Springs and Papoose Lake. They are on the divide of several drainages that flow in opposite directions. Great country to test your ability to get lost!

At that point in time I had only a very basic idea of the directions these streams flowed, what their names were, or what would be the next drainage that they would flow into. We had no maps or compass. These were for sissies!

All the survival books and information instructed a person to go down stream and you would run into some kind of civilization, eventually. That is probably correct but with a lifetime only being so long you could hasten your departure by starving to death prior to this encounter with civilization.

Luckily, my dad had been turned around a few times in his life, (as in lost!) He had learned the fallacies of the downstream method and told me, "Stan, memorize landmarks and if you get turned around, go uphill to the highest point you can find and wait out storms or whatever until you can locate your land mark".

He walked from Mackay, Idaho to Armstead, Montana when he was 16 years old trying to find a job, said he was lost the whole trip!

Studying maps later I found that from the Coyote Springs area, Papoose Creek flows easterly toward the Middle Fork of the Salmon River and Impassable Canyon – no trail down Papoose and no trail down the Middle Fork until it reaches the main Salmon River some 24 miles away.

Cave Creek flows southerly toward Big Creek, about ten miles away. Iodine Creek flows westerly and Farrow Creek flows northerly toward the Salmon River with very few trails.

There was at least two feet of snow on the ground. The elk tracks that we found seemed to be coming out of the drainages to the west and north at night, feeding in the meadows and hillsides at the head of Papoose Creek and then returning to the drainages to the west and north that I now know are Iodine Creek and Farrow Creek. Because we were never able to catch the elk out on our side we developed one of the "dreaded plans"!

Jerry and Lawrence would position themselves on the ridge top at what later was determined to be the head of Farrow Creek. Gerald and I would take our saddle horses down Iodine Creek a couple of miles, cross over the ridge to the north into the later identified Farrow Creek and then being positive that we had encircled all the elk in that part of Idaho – we would come shooting and shouting up the Farrow drainage toward Jerry and Lawrence and they would thereby "Reduce their elk to possession!" "Is that the next perfect plan or what?"

We could possibly have picked a better day for its execution. It was snowing very hard and the fog was so thick that the best of visibility might have stretched to fifty yards.

Gerald and I were leading our horses down a very steep (as in precipitous) hillside when a herd of elk materialized around us and crashed down the hill in the wrong direction to coincide with "the plan."

Gerald dropped his reins and hollered back "Bring my horse, I'll head them off!"

I kept descending the hill following the running elk tracks, riding my horse, leading Geralds, finally crossing the creek and after another half mile or so caught up to Gerald. This elk herd had not played by the rules of the "plan" and would live to outsmart us another day. It was still so foggy that you couldn't see the tops of the trees. We mounted up and started riding with Gerald in the lead. He had been in the area hunting a couple of times before.

We were now entering some pretty ouchy terrain, big rocks, shale slides, down logs, etc. I felt we were going about 180 degrees in the wrong direction but assumed Gerald was trying to find a way around this mess we were in.

It was now starting toward darkness when we got by the really bad stuff and I assumed Gerald would turn back to the right and toward the head of the main canyon. However, he continued in the same direction.

I asked him, “Where are we headed?”

“Up here to Jerry and Lawrence.”

“Man, they aren’t this way; they are more nearly behind us now.”

I was a teenager, pretty new to this kind of terrain. Gerald was a man of probably fifty years with lots of mountain experience.

A possible dilemma could be in the second stages of development. I could sense a small amount of doubt in his voice as he replied,

“Let’s shoot a couple of times, maybe they will answer us.”

“Gerald, we’re supposed to be down here making noise to run the elk up. They won’t answer us.”

“Let’s try.”

I shot a couple of shots with my 30-06 Springfield into a dead stump. The ensuing silence bordered on deafening! Our horses were pretty well beat from plowing the deep snow and fighting the bad terrain.

I said “Gerald, I think you got turned around running through the fog, and back and forth across the creek, trying to turn that elk herd back.” “I think I’m right because of my pretty much straight line and only one creek crossing.”

“I will make you a deal, Gerald. If you will follow me until it is too dark to see and I haven’t got us out of this, I will shut up and follow you from then on.”

I was riding a small, red, pinto, three year old mare named Fanny that was pretty tired. I picked the best route I could find in the direction I felt we had to go and stopped to rest every few yards to give the horses every chance to keep what power they had left. Just at final darkness we rode into the trees where Jerry and Lawrence were waiting. Good feeling? You bet your sweet biffey!

That was Gerald's first "turnaround". And many, many years later he was still trying to piece together how he could have gotten disoriented.

I learned a lot from Lawrence Halverson regarding the salvage of an elk. Up till then I would just cut the head off and bring the rest of the carcass back to camp. Wrong! The head came back, was skinned out, the tongue removed and boiled for lunch meat, and the brains taken out to fry with the eggs for breakfast. The jaws and all meat was boned from the head and neck for stew meat.

The magpies, ravens and coyotes didn't fare all that well after we took care of an elk "the Lawrence way."

## I'd Been Lost with Someone Else -- Now to Practice by Myself

Having been with a pretty well practiced mountain man when he got turned around I pretty well knew my time would probably someday come.

Sure enough! Joy, my dad and I had purchased an outfitting business in Chamberlain Basin. This is probably 30 miles west of the country we were hunting when Gerald got turned around in the fog. Note the word fog. It was once again going to be the lead player in my turn-around.

We bought the outfit in early August of 1963. As part of the purchase agreement, the guy we bought it from would help us set up all the hunting camps, show us the area boundary and guide for us the first fall.

None of this happened and we had to find the location of the camps, set them up, and learn the area as we hunted. Not a smooth indoctrination by a long ways.

The base of operations was an old cabin at the Hotzel Ranch; we had negotiated a lease with the Idaho Fish and Game Department that owned it. The ranch and meadow were to the east end of the Chamberlain airstrip.

We had muffed and bluffed our way through most of the season but had one more hunt booked in mid-November, before we could pull out with the horses and mules.

That hunt would start in a few days and we were set up and ready, so Joy and I decided to see if we could get our own elk and learn some more of the area closer to the ranch.

We hiked across the meadow on the trail to Moose Meadows and the Root Ranch. There were fresh elk tracks scattered along the trail but Joy had a bad cold and couldn't keep from coughing and scaring the elk.

We went up to the Lodgepole Lookout which was a little tower on the top of a tall tree. From there we could see the cabin at the ranch. I told Joy to wait a few hours and if I wasn't back by 3:00pm then to hunt back to the cabin.

I would hunt to the south along the trail toward Moose Meadows and swing to the left and back towards her. I crossed Lodgepole Creek and went on for a couple miles. It then started to snow and the fog moved in. About then I jumped some elk and spent a couple hours chasing them back and fourth through the thick trees and fog. I finally decided they had won so I headed for home.

I dropped into a drainage I assumed would have a stream running to my right – should be Lodgepole Creek, but the stream is running to my left! Bang! Now you're trying to replay the elk chase in the fog, through springs, meadows, swamps and hillsides to see if you can get re-orientated.

Nothing would come together. I fell through the ice and got wet.

I then came to an abandoned hunter's camp that I could tell had been used only a few weeks before. There was a pint bottle of stick matches and a can of consommé soup stuck in the fork of a tree. I added some matches to my waterproof match kit and drank the soup cold.

I still couldn't tell myself where I was. After another hour or so of travel, the vegetation started changing from fir and lodgepole pine to ponderosa and with some mountain mahogany starting to show up.

I knew then I was headed toward the Salmon River which definitely was not where I wanted to go.

I then headed up, probably climbing fifteen hundred feet or so, to a ridge top where I knew I would be able to see something when the storm ended and the fog dissipated.

I built a good fire where I could dry out – between falling through the ice and exerting myself pretty hard – I was as wet as the proverbial "Drowned Rat". I toasted my last sandwich over the fire and dried out and was able to get some good rest.

In another hour or so the storm started to abate and an occasional hole in the fog and clouds would appear.

Finally, through one of the small holes in the clouds and fog I saw an open grassy mountain top with a lookout tower on top. I recognized it from flying over as Grass Mountain Lookout.

I knew then what I had to do to get home. Drop down to Chamberlain Creek and go up it to the ranch. It would only be about twelve miles from where I would hit Chamberlain Creek.

It got dark about the time I hit the creek and trail but I was in good shape and trotted up the creek for two or three hours to the cabin where I knew Joy would be nervously waiting. I tell you, that lantern light was a very welcome sight.

**THE OLD HOTZEL CABIN IN CHAMBERLAIN BASIN WHERE THE LANTERN LIGHT LOOKED SO GOOD AFTER MY EXTENDED "WALKABOUT". (CABIN BURNED DOWN IN YEAR 2000 FOREST FIRE.)**

After a good night's sleep I got out the map and, as nearly as I could retrace my little journey, I found I had covered about thirty four air miles with nearly half of it without benefit of any kind of trail.

I was telling this story to Gilman Martiny. He said he and Bill Sullivan had been wandering around in this same part of the world and not real sure where they were for a couple of days. He said Bill hollered back to him, "We're saved – we're saved!"

Gilman said Bill had found a tree with one of their old friend's (who wasn't much of a mountain man) name carved in the bark.

Bill said, “If that dumb S.O.B. found his way out of here we can too”.

Also, Gilman told me his sure fire way of getting rescued if he thought he was really lost.

“Just shoot a couple of shots and within ten minutes a game warden will show up and you can then follow him out!”

I think Gilman may have actually used this system a few times, either intentionally or accidentally!

# *Chapter 13*

# Can Chukars Swim? Plus several sub-chapters on other probably useless, but possibly interesting information.

## Can Chukars Swim?

You probably have never considered the answer to this question. I know I never had until the following incident unfolded. I was riding along the Middle Fork of the Salmon River trail just below the mouth of Rattlesnake Creek, (they could have named all the creeks in there Rattlesnake and they would have been very correct)!

The trail is on the east side of the river and I was headed to the north and downstream. The terrain is very steep and some of the places you can literally touch the rocks at the side of the trail.

The river varies in width but around three hundred feet would be an average and it was about this wide where the great chukar swim unfolded!

It was a hot September afternoon as I came around one of the cliffs that the trail had been carved into. In a slight rocky indentation in the shade a chukar rested -- probably dreaming of the fat grass hoppers he, she, it?, would soon be catching as the afternoon cooled enough for it to go ahunting. The chukar's reverie was interrupted by yours truly and his clattering packstring.

The chukar roared out of its shady nook and across the river. Alas, I'm afraid it had not had time to become properly awakened or its' altimeter was off a few feet. For whatever reason, it flew into the water about midway across.

Having never witnessed something like this and knowing the anatomy of a chukar was not overly conducive to being the Mark Spitz of the avian world - I pulled my packstring to a halt to watch another of nature's events unfold.

El chukar surfaced and with about one fourth of his body above water continued onward – now swimming slowly on across the river, or at least hopefully across. I could tell he was really having problems.

**CHUKAR**
**NOTE: FEET NOT DESIGNED FOR SWIMMING!**

It probably was at least five minutes later and a couple hundred yards farther down the river before it reached the far side and – naturally no smooth gradual sandbar to crawl out of the river onto. No! big rocks and rough terrain.

I was now off my horse and watching through the binoculars to see what would one way or another, be the end of the movie.

The poor little guy was pretty well spent (as in absolutely pooped)! It would reach up with its beak and pull with all its might. I could see the little water logged wings fluttering for all they were worth and I'm sure the un-webbed feet were also digging for a toe hold of any kind.

She, he, it, would lose its purchase, be forced downstream a few feet by the flow of the current and then try again. Finally, a try was made at a spot that exhibited a little better chance of a successful conclusion.

The little beak found a beak hold, the little feet found some feet holds and the little water logged body broke loose from the tension of the water and onto a flat rock a few inches above the lapping of the water.

Through the binoculars I could almost feel the relief emanating from the bedraggled little body – "Man, I'm not going to try that again!"

An addendum to this chukar story happened in Nevada, at a place on Salmon Falls Creek called Burnt Meadows.

Joy and I and our dog Freckles were hunting chukar. I watched a bunch, covey, group or herd, fly down to the creek for a drink of water. I skulked down within range and when they flew I shot two of them that landed in the rocks across the creek. Freckles and I crossed over and she retrieved the birds for me.

When she delivered the second one, I looked at them, and couldn't believe my eyes. They had webbed feet!

Evidently, some teal were swimming in the creek at the spot the chukars were getting a drink. When the birds flew all up together; I succeeded in dropping two teal from a covey of chukar!

One more claim to fame! Doing something no one else has ever done.

## The First Two of Many Ambulance Rides in the Last Fifty + Years!

In the spring of 1953, while attending the University of Idaho in Moscow I traveled over to Yakima, Washington to a rodeo.

I was on the Rodeo Team at the U of I, but there wasn't a College rodeo every weekend. On weekends that there were no College rodeos I would look for a rodeo within driving distance.

The reason was twofold, a chance to practice plus a chance to win some money.

The Yakima Rodeo was a professional rodeo sanctioned by what was then called the Rodeo Cowboys of America. A forerunner of the Professional Rodeo Cowboys of America (PRCA), as it is called today.

The rodeo stock was furnished by Joe Kelsey, one of the northwest's premier rodeo contractors. He had some good ones and I drew one that might have been somewhat "Gooder" than the rest.

The lady bareback horse was called "The Black Widow" and she catapulted the Idaho cowboy over her head midway through the proposed eight second ride and then kicked me in the head as she passed over me.

I had a brand new Fox© Hat on that probably saved my life. The brim took the force of her hind foot and folded against the crown.

Her hoof cut about a four inch slash in the brim, about a three inch cut in the crown and about a two inch cut in the Potts noggin!

Fortunately I was kicked in the head or I could have been seriously injured!

They carted me out in the ambulance and I told the doctor type people to just bandage it as I was up in the Steer Wrestling next.

I don't know if I was still a little woozy from the head kick but I succeeded in missing my steer and taking a spectacular header in the rocky Yakima arena.

Yep, ambulance was back for me! It was as if I had my own private ambulance. They got me patched up and now we had to head for home.

The money I was going to win was now in somebody else's pocket.

My buddy Gene Kemp from high school days had a 1941 Ford sedan that was our wheels. We gassed it up prior to starting home. Possibly the smartest thing we did on the whole trip.

I had twenty bucks; I knew where there was a poker game, so the money that would not come my way in the rodeo arena would roll my way across the green felt table top, right!

Wrong, those old apple farmers new a pigeon when he flew in and plucked this one's feathers like a Thanksgiving turkey!

So with Kemp the driver and us now broke, I told him to take us home.

It was the middle of the night when we headed back for Moscow. Somehow, Gene got headed the wrong way and it was about daylight when we came back through Yakima! Good thing the old Ford got good mileage! Another typical, successful, rodeo trip!

## Shooting a Tree in Two with a 30-30

Now that I have added to your stock of useless information by showing you that a chukar can swim – I will enhance you farther by telling of bisecting a tree with rifle bullets!

One summer, while I was living in Hailey, Idaho, and outfitting in the Idaho Wilderness area, I loaded a trailer load of horses, some camp gear and horse feed, a few groceries, a little beer and whiskey and headed over Galena Summit, through Stanley, Idaho and down the Salmon River towards the Stoddard Trail Head, some two hundred miles away.

The purpose of the trip was to clear some trails and cut some firewood for the fall hunting season. It was evening time when I drove into the little town of Challis, Idaho.

Having more friends than enemies that hung around the local watering holes and gin clinics, I decided to stop and have a beer or two as I visited my way around the village.

At one stop, I think it was the Custer Saloon or the Campfire Bar, I ran into my old friend Con Hourihan. I had sold him an outfitting business several years before but somehow he was still my friend.

I told him of my planned trip and began embellishing the journey with tales of the beautiful scenery, giant trout that lived in the lakes, giant big horn rams and mule deer bucks I would be seeing, and if I got bored with fishing and sightseeing I might clear some trail and cut a few blocks of firewood.

As the beers continued to flow I could see that the snare was gradually tightening – "Why, Hell yes, I'd be glad to have someone to visit with and share the vistas and tranquility that would await us."

Con said, "My wife is in Nevada visiting her folks – I'll be glad to come along."

The snare had tightened, the trap had sprung, and the deadfall had dropped! I had, to say the least, put the "con on Con!"

We gathered his saddle and bed roll and toward morning continued on down the river to the trail head where we would trade our gas horsepower for horse and mule power.

Part way into the Cradle Creek Camp we were going down the switchbacks into Reese Creek. I was in the lead and Con behind when he whistled, "Man! Look at the size of that buck."

I looked up through the trees in the direction he was pointing and there was a doe and a little four point mule deer buck. My first thought was, "Boy, old Con had too mas cerveza – his vision is still bad!"

About then, around a tree came a giant mule deer buck, wide of spread and many of points. This was late June and he was in velvet but with horns fully developed. A dream buck if we could find him in the fall. (We didn't.)

We continued on to Cradle Creek, unloaded most of our camp, grazed the stock and spent the night. We then took the fishing gear and a little camp and headed for Stoddard Lake.

We could see some snow on the top of Stoddard Peak but when we got to the last few hundred yards the snow and drifts were too deep for the stock to get through.

We continued on foot, out to where we could see the first lake. It was still frozen over, with snow slides, rocks and trees on the ice. It was nearly the Fourth of July and still winter up here.

I wanted to do some exploring so I told Con where I would meet him (the trail crossing on the Main Fork of Papoose Creek). I would cross country it, looking for new ram, elk and deer hunting country.

It was dark when I got there, Con had a big fire; we had some supper, grazed the horses and bedded down for the night.

Next morning I found we had camped by the same tree the old guys had camped under when they brought me into the country some forty years before!

The main Papoose Creek was so high, with high water; it would have been suicide to even try a crossing, so we went back to Cradle Camp, to the "Cut a few blocks of wood" game.

When we got organized for our little wood cutting venture, we found the only good dry tree anywhere close was about fifty yards below camp. It had blown over but the top had hung up in another tree. It had a tremendous bend in it with obviously lots of torque. However, with only a six foot "misery whip" there was no way to safely cut it so it would fall and break away from the other tree. The bottom was just too vertical. It would have been simple with a chain saw but that is a no-no in the wilderness.

I hereby had one of my dreaded "Strokes of Genius." We'll shoot it down!

The ponderosa was probably between two and three feet thru at ground level but up there near where it was hung in the crotch it was only about one foot in diameter.

My fire power was a Winchester Model 94 in 30-30 caliber along with seven or eight "Catriges." (This word is from my old friend Captain Ben Hurtig. I went to his funeral last week.) I got my spotter, Con, behind me with the binoculars to call my shots.

There was a small knot that appeared to be about one inch across in the sharpest part of the bend. My plan, "Ha-Ha" once again "Plan," was to shoot the knot, then an inch on each side of it until the pressure of the leaning tree broke it and it would come to the ground so we could start bucking it up into stove lengths.

I told Con my "Plan," got a solid rest over a tree stump and fired the first "Catrige."

Con said, "You missed the knot, I can't even see where you hit."

I borrowed the binoculars and could see the hole right at the edge of the knot.

I shot again -- same response from my spotter.

I looked. A hole on the other side of knot.

After about the fourth shot we finally got our signals together. I was shooting at one knot and Con was looking at another one about three feet away.

Now, I am about half out of "Catriges" with no visible sign of the "Plan" working. We couldn't see the back side of the tree but I knew the bullets should be going through or nearly through and had to be weakening the tree.

I can not remember exactly, but I think I only had one or two more chances and we were discussing further options when a small breeze came up, the tree broke and down it came!

I'm going to take the credit even if the tree only fell because of

**THE CRADLE CREEK CAMP**
**SCENE OF THE 30-30 LOGGING EXPERIMENT!**

the wind! Claim to fame number two!

## Cactus Pete's and the Check Cashing Card

The year after Joy and I bought the ranch in Nevada the country went into a major drought.

I had bought some hay in Idaho and my neighbors Daryl Weeks and Vernon Dalton were helping me haul it. We would stop at a new casino called Cactus Pete's just inside the Nevada border for supper on some of these trips.

One night I needed to cash a check and they told us they could cash one once, but we should get a check cashing card for the next time. Usually a big check might have been twenty five dollars but for some reason I wrote "Five hundred dollars" on the line for the maximum amount of checks in one night.

A month or so later I needed to cash another check, wrote it out for twenty five dollars for supper and was informed they couldn't cash it because I had exceeded my five hundred dollars! I got a hold of the manager to try and find out what had happened. Ultimately, it boiled down to forgery.

An Indian kid that had gone to the same high school I attended, in Mackay, Idaho, had written enough counter checks on my account to wipe out my five hundred dollars!

My signature card was on file and the signature was not even close. If I remember right, he hadn't even spelled my name right. He tried it again and this time they caught him and he went up the creek for awhile.

However, it caused enough of a problem to cash a check at Cactus Pete's that I just gave it up.

## Another Potential Moneymaker
## Selling Spuds in Anaconda, Montana

In about February of one of the early years of our commercial potato growing ventures, Joy's uncle, Buddy Blume from Anaconda, Montana dropped by while we were sorting potatoes.

The sorting tables are endless conveyor belts that move the potatoes along at an adjustable speed.

The tables were approximately three feet wide and ten feet long and have from four to eight people standing along the edges watching the potatoes move slowly along. The sorter's job is to make sure the potatoes that go over the end to be bagged fall within the government grade that the grower is striving for.

Some U.S. # 1 grades used were: two inch minimum, six ounce minimum, eight ounce minimum, ten ounce minimum and strictly bakers.

The potatoes were also certified for seed potatoes by the Idaho Crop Improvement Association.

This gave us several different options to market our potatoes.

When the potatoes were scooped out of a bulk pile they moved up a rubber covered endless conveyor belt and were dropped onto some revolving hard rubber vibrating rods called eliminators that could have the space between them changed to let the smaller ones – under two inches in diameter drop through.

This let them go along a separate tray and into sacks for strictly seed potatoes. This left fewer potatoes to look at as the # 1's for eating potatoes moved along the center of the table.

No more than three percent of a bag of #1 potato's could fall outside of the government inspection tolerance.

Number two grade potatoes were usually somewhat misshapen with knobby protrusions called knots. These were hand moved to another divider and were sacked as # 2's at a lower price.

After the potatoes were sorted and bagged they were stacked until there were enough sacks to fill a refrigerated rail car.

Before they were loaded or during the loading process the government inspectors would look at several random sacks to make sure they were within tolerance.

If they were not – the entire car load had to be resorted.

Therefore, we were very careful to ensure the potatoes were sorted correctly.

Now, this particular year, as in most of the years we raised potatoes, the prices for all grades including seed potatoes, were very low.

Joy's Uncle Buddy watched us sort these beautiful potatoes that were being shipped at a price that barely broke us even.

He said, "Let me take a sack of these back to the grocery store in Anaconda. I think they would be interested. These are much nicer potatoes than they sell."

Anaconda, Montana at that point in history was still a big copper mining and smelting town, owned and operated by The Anaconda Copper Company.

Buddy called me back in a few days with the good news. Yes, the store would like a truck load of 160 sacks every week at a price about three times what we were getting!

All right! There will never be another poor day!

Wrong! We hauled two loads up and had the third ready to go when the store owner called.

The mine and mill had gone on strike – everyone was out of work and he couldn't take any more spuds till it was settled.

That took several months and I sold the last 10,000 sacks for $.20 (Yes!) Twenty cents per hundred and the check bounced!

## One Mad Cop!

This is a very short story about one very mad officer of the law. It happened thusly.

I was in San Francisco, many years ago, at the sports and boat show at the Cow Palace. I was driving somewhere over on the ocean side trying to locate the home of one of my clients.

I had pulled up to a four way intersection with a policeman out in the center directing traffic. I cannot remember if the traffic lights weren't operating or if the human traffic signal was normal operating procedure. No matter, he would send a few vehicles from one street though, then the next and so on.

Some would go straight; some would turn right and some left. I didn't see the entire incident. I am relating only the final result so will do my best to explain what I think happened.

I was on one side of the intersection; the policeman was directing the traffic flow directly across from me. The last car in the group he was controlling was making a left turn just as the policeman turned to direct the next group.

Somehow the left turning vehicle hit the policeman probably doing six or eight miles per hour and stopped with the policeman lying on the hood!

Whether the policeman jumped (probably), or was just tall enough to fall on the hood, I can't say. What I am sure of is he was more than moderately agitated!

The cop is belly down on the hood, head right against the windshield looking at the poor SHMOO that tapped him and reading him the riot act. He was beating on the hood, discussing the drivers heritage and possible future at the top of his lungs!

He then got off and with his head through the side window continued the same. Poor driver! I wish I could draw so I could give you the look on both their faces.

You will just have to imagine it and like me, be thankful the policeman wasn't hurt.

# Chapter 14

# Mining at Wildhorse

In the winter of 1955 and 1956, being twenty years old, fairly newly married and badly broke (as usual) I was able to get a job about fifty miles from our little farm on the Houston Lane near Mackay, Idaho.

I could work five days and then come home for a couple of days. Joy would keep the home fires burning (an absolute necessity).

Our house was an old log model with an excellent ventilation system (as the wind blew through and actually drifted snow on the floor!). The bathroom nay, outhouse was only a brisk forty yard hike through snow drifts of usually only moderate depth.

At least we had running water. It ran by in the creek which was only the distance of a average rifle shot at a deer away. The ice seldom froze more than four or five inches thick in any one night.

In addition, she would care for (as in feed and water) our small covey of assorted livestock and poultry. The covey consisted of about ten cows, three or four horses, three or four hogs, about one hundred sheep, a few laying hens and a few turkeys. But, on with more of the brighter spots of our existence. Our daughter Kay was now a long yearling.

Joy and Kay had gone to town for groceries. When they returned, Joy brought Kay in the house and set her on the couch while she packed in the groceries.

On the first grocery run, Kay said, "Big mouse, mom!" With the second load a giant pack rat ran across the room! Yah- big mouse is right!

Joy and I had taken up square dancing. We would go to someone's house every Saturday night. Worth Ivie would call the squares and along towards morning we'd have a big feed and everyone would head for home to do the morning chores.

About once a month we would go to Arco, twenty eight miles down the valley and square dance there and on alternate months they would come to Mackay.

For Joy's birthday I had splurged and bought her a beautiful turquoise, brown and fawn colored squaw dress for the dances.

**THE MILL AREA AT WILDHORSE MINE ABOUT 15 YEARS AGO. PHOTO OF FAMILY PICNIC.**

(I'm not sure what the political or ethical name for the dress would be today but probably something like, "Indian Female of the Southwest dress.")

She had only worn it once when a typical "Potts" disaster struck. Somehow, one of the hogs had pushed the door open and ripped, tore, shredded and virtually destroyed Joy's birthday present.

The hog was actually pretty tasty if you could take a bite without thinking about the dress!

Several of the local ranchers and their wives along with guys from town were working at the Wildhorse Mine also. Car pools of four or five people were the norm with drivers trading off each trip.

Some of the workers I remember working there when I did were, Gerald and Minerva Twitchell, Don Ivie, Howard Rosenkrantz, Joe Rukavina, Stan and Lewis Johnson, Wiley and Marie Krebetts, Pete Peterson, "Pinochle" Selander, Richard Park, Leroy Ivie and Ferrell Larter.

The mine was primarily recovering a type of tungsten ore called sheelite. The mine was owned by a company called Cordera Mining Company which was a subsidiary of Sun Oil Company.

The company had constructed a mill, bunk house and cook house so it was a small close knit community covering two or three acres. With the ore recovery areas off in several directions and mostly open pit, but with at least one drift (tunnel), being developed. In miners slang these are called "Diggins."

I worked there several months until spring had returned to Lost River Valley and spring planting and lambing time had arrived.

The mill operated twenty-four hours a day. It was a flotation mill and used several hundred gallons of water per minute.

The rocks, with the ore inside, were hauled with small two-ton size dump trucks to a flat area above the mill. There the rocks were stock piled until needed and then pushed with a TD 14 International© Dozer to what they call a "grizzly."

A grizzly is constructed of heavy railroad rails spaced the proper distance apart on an incline of probably forty five degrees and welded. The rocks that fall through are small enough to go through the crusher. Rocks that were too large had to be reduced in size with a heavy sledge hammer. Not the most sought after job THERE!

After the rock passed through the crusher it was reduced to a fine dust that was washed over the vibrating floatation tables that slope very gradually in two directions – both forward and sideways.

There are baffles on the surface of the tables and as the water mixture called slurry passes over the table, the concentrated ore called "cons," which is much heavier than the rock called "waste," works its way to the lower side and is funneled into a separate chute where it is sacked and moved to the dryer.

The mill operators had to be very vigilant and precise with their adjustments of slope and water flow to prevent more than minimal loss of the "cons."

The sheelite shines or glows, under infrared and ultra violet light and a "black light" was used in darkened conditions to monitor the ore/waste separation. A very exacting job and a good mill operator was worth his weight in gold. A small amount of waste had to be funneled into the "cons," but the ideal was at least sixty percent pure sheelite.

When at least twelve tons of "cons" were dried the sacks were loaded on larger trucks and hauled to the rail head in Mackay or sometimes on to Final Milling Refinement in Utah.

The Wildhorse mine was located in a narrow (three hundred feet wide,) high elevation (eight thousand foot) valley with Wildhorse

Creek about eight foot wide and one foot deep coming down the bottom of the canyon.

The water for the mill was pumped via a centrifugal pump to the mill, cookhouse, bunkhouse etc. The miners, truck drivers, cat skinners, carpenters, shovel operators and timber men usually worked only during daylight hours.

The sheelite – tungsten ore when refined was used in the hardening of steel and in electrical filaments, etc. It has a melting point of 3410◦ C.

Nearly all the employees had to be able to work at several different jobs – depending on where they were needed.

I primarily drove truck, operated one of the dozers, worked with one of the drilling crews operating a jack-leg drill or on what they call a wagon drill, drilling and blasting the rock. Occasionally, I would help in the mill as a mill hand and sometimes would get stuck on the grizzly with the twelve pound sledge making "little ones out of big ones!"

When we would get into a vein of very highly concentrated minerals the bosses would change the "modus-operandi" somewhat.

After a round had been blasted, Howard Rosenkrantz and I would become "hi-graders," and would work the "muck pile" by hand with the black light. We had a little TD9 International © loader and a Dodge© 1 ½ ton dump truck.

We would shine the muck pile (blasted rock) with the black lights. The high grade rocks would shine brightly in a whitish/chartreuse green color. We would manually place these nearly pure rocks, whether golf ball size or watermelon size in the bucket of the TD9 and when full, dump it into the dump truck.

This way the "hi-grade" stayed separate from the regular run of ore and went to the Final milling process just as it came out of the ground. Sometimes it would take a couple of nights to fill the dump truck.

Now the roads we used were not developed at all past the stage of smoothing with a dozer blade. Also, the terrain, being so steep, didn't lend itself to the development of nice wide curves at the switchbacks.

There were three different types of curves – 1) the rare curve wide enough to turn the truck and be able to go the next direction. 2) the curve that could be negotiated with only one back up to make the corner and 3) a few weren't curves at all but just places you pulled up one switchback, backed the truck up the next grade – pulled forward on the third until you finally (hopefully) got to where you were headed.

Because of the risky nature of this, we took the doors off both sides of the cab so in the event of a possible, potential, probable, catastrophe, you MIGHT be able to bail out and save your skin!

All the above trivial information is a lead-in to a few hair raising, harum-scarum, pulse quickening and virtually terrifying experiences that happened to yours truly, in that short period of time!

## Wild Ride Number One

On one trip down the mountain, with a loaded ore truck, a couple of the miners wanted a ride down to the mill with me so they crawled in the no door Dodge.©

Now, with a loaded ore truck in that type of situation, speed is the last thing on your priority list.

You have it in the bottom of all gears available. i.e. "The Big Hole" as it is known in truck driver parlance. The engine is screaming like a convention of banshees, the tachometer is near the red line even with the occasional tapping of the brakes and we approached the first direction change, a curve number two, at a speed probably near two miles per hour. It was a left hand #2 so in the ideal scenario you would cut the steering wheel sharp left until the front wheels were nearly to the vertical drop off, stop, shift to reverse, back up while cutting wheels full right, stop again, cut the wheels full left again and hopefully maneuver said curve number two.

You noticed I labeled that as the ideal scenario. On this day it was not ideal. The not–so-ideal scenario played as follows. I entered the initial left hand portion of the turn and was probably ten feet from the vertical drop off when silence, and the truck hurtled forward! "Continued Next Month!"

Now the two old miners (forty five or fifty then), abandoned ship like they had been shot from a boomerang! The truck driver, me, nearly drove the brake pedal through the floor boards as it slid to a stop with the front wheels actually starting over the edge!

Now what! I'm stopped and cannot move, I have no idea what happened. My "companeros," the miners, were still nearby so I started barking orders. Get the big, bigger and biggest rocks you can find and wedge them in front of the rear tires.

It probably took twenty or more minutes for them to get a rock pile built up nearly to the dump bed – probably three feet high. My brake leg was about worn out by then but it was test time. I gradually released the pressure and the truck held!

I vaulted, leapt, nay, stumbled out and after moving around until I had a little strength in my legs, I crawled under the truck, just a little way to where I could try to see what had happened. The rear end of the drive shaft was lying on the ground!

When we got back with some big equipment to anchor and fix the problem we found that the center pin, a bolt that goes up through the frame and the springs had broken and let the rear axle move backwards a couple of inches and disconnected the drive shaft.

It was nearly, "Wake up Leroy! You ain't never seen a wreck like this one's gonna be."

It was probably three hundred feet nearly straight down to the next road and six or eight hundred feet to the bottom of the canyon.

## The Freeze Up

Along about February we had a cold spell like -30° and -40° for a few nights – would warm up to only -20° during the day.

The centrifugal pump, pumped the water out of a small pond in the creek. The discharge pressure was probably at least 80 PSI.

One day it dropped to 50 below zero and actually reduced the discharge pipe with ice until it became solid. For several days we could do nothing except cut more wood for the stoves to keep warm.

## Wild Ride Number Two

The fuel tanks to fill the equipment were at the lower end of a parking lot that was located between the mill and the creek. The area where the ore was stock piled above the "grizzly" was accessed by a straight road on a gradual, for that country, grade.

The TD14 was getting low on fuel one day so I decided to take it down and fuel it up. The road was getting pretty icy. The TD 14 did not have ice "grousers." Grousers are small iron strips welded cross ways of the pads to keep a machine from sliding sideways on an icy slope! As long as the machine is vertical to the slope the risers on the pads hold it back.

As I found out, it only takes the most gentle of slopes to cause a very speedy run-a-way. I pulled across the level ore stock pile area to the road and started to turn down toward the fuel tanks. I thought it was still level but obviously, it wasn't.

A docile slow moving piece of machinery became a hurdling twelve ton ice-skate in less than a blink of an eye. The parking lot was partially full with pickups, assorted equipment and the fuel tanks.

I went down through there fifty or sixty yards and to a stop in probably no more than ten seconds. I had manipulated friction clutches, brakes, throttle all to no avail.

It stopped, I got off, looked around for any spectators or damage to parked vehicles. No damage and as near as I can tell – no spectators, as in shift bosses, foremen, superintendent or owners.

I pulled it over – fueled it up and went back straight up the road with no one the wiser - except hopefully me.

If it had happened where there was only air at the bottom, instead of a flat stopping spot, this story probably would not have been written – at least not by me.

I was seriously trying to get off of the tractor, during most of the time it was in the slide and when it stopped I was sitting flat in the seat! So much for being young, agile and active.

## Tip Up!

Ride number THREE, the dump truck end gates can be dropped from the top or bottom. The bottom is released from a lever accessed just behind the cab. Used for dirt, gravel and rocks smaller than a couple of feet in diameter.

To drop them from the top – a pin must be pulled on both sides on top. This is used for rocks to big to go through the gate. This is to keep a big rock from wedging in the gate and tipping the truck over backwards.

I found out the hard way that dumping any kind of medium sized rocks with the top of the dump closed is Very Dangerous.

What happens is, two of the rocks wedge and the load slides to the back and, overbalances the truck because the load can't slide off.

It's a weird feeling as the front of the truck which is horizontal to the ground goes up in the air about fifteen feet and is vertical!

You then have to get some kind of equipment to unravel your mess. Live and, hopefully, learn!

# Chapter 15

# Perrine Bridge

Not everyone that crosses the Perrine Bridge should have this much excitement!

**READ ON FOR THE POTTS FACTOR EXCITEMENT.
"BISBEE" PHOTO TAKEN DURING BRIDGE CONSTRUCTION**

Near Twin Falls, Idaho is a bridge that crosses the Snake River and is to say the very least, quite impressive.

It is higher from the water than Niagara Falls, 486 feet and 1500 feet across and is named the Perrine Bridge. Highway 93, the major north-south highway in this area crosses here.

In 2006 it is four lanes wide with steel and concrete sides about five feet high, but thirty years ago it was only two narrow lanes with about a three foot guardrail.

From the bridge you can see the spot that Evil Knievel tried his infamous rocket motorcycle jump. For sheer spectator excitement his attempt to jump the river was probably more lasting but the "Pucker Factor" in my little escapade would have ranked a strong 10!

When the original bridge was constructed in 1927 it was the highest in the world. I will try to lay out the scenario – I hope in a manner that will give you a feel for the happenings.

I was northbound – headed from my ranch in Wells, Nevada to Meyers Cove, north of Challis, Idaho. I was driving a ¾ ton Ford pickup and towing a double axle, 18 foot, Bucko© trailer loaded with twelve of my mules for part of the packstring at the hunting camp Joy and I operated out of the Taylor Ranch on Big Creek.

At about the center of the bridge I felt the pickup suddenly drop down on the left rear accompanied by a loud bang and great quantities of sparks shooting out from underneath.

A car had just passed me going south and another was fast approaching. In the mirror I saw the left rear wheel with about a two foot axle stub roll across the incoming traffic lane just behind the car I had just passed.

It hit the guardrail. Bounced and ricochet back over the car that was now going by and toward and then under my rapidly decelerating pickup and trailer! This was only three or four feet in front of the next approaching vehicle!

All this was accompanied still by the great screeching noise of metal sliding on cement and still throwing a huge shower of sparks behind me and into the incoming lane of traffic. By now my machinery had skidded to a stop but the wheel and axle stub had ended up under the trailer with the sharp hub puncturing tires.

The guys in the car that the wheel and stub had just missed stopped to see if they could help. I told him "Yes, get to the closest phone – call the highway patrol and a big wrecker for me."

There was one lane open for traffic so I started directing and moving the trucks and autos past as best I could. In a very few minutes, probably over five but less than ten, here came a wrecker with dollies accompanied by a highway patrolman.

They got the trailer and pickup jacked up and on the dolly. They then eased my rig on across the bridge and out of the traffic flow. About then was probably the first deep breath I was able to draw!

The wrecker towed my pickup to a garage, I got the tires repaired and replaced and was back on the road within three or four hours – a great ending to what could have been a really bad problem.

# Chapter 16

# The $80,000 Painting

No, I'm not a collector of high dollar paintings but this story has worked its way into, "The Potts Factor/Murphy's Law," listing of one more memorable but not pleasurable memories.

It plays out as follows; around 1981 the town of Challis was in the early stages of one of its mining booms. Property values were soaring, rental properties were at a premium because of a lack of housing for the several hundred mine employees.

Not the choicest period to wander into town looking for property, right? Hey! We're dealing with "The Potts Factor" here.

I had recently finished a residential subdivision in the town of Hailey that had proven the "Potts Factor" still alive and well. In other words it worked its way into an unsuccessful, non-producing, money hemorrhaging status. I had some lots that were free and clear but even by reducing the price to one-half of what they had been selling for a couple of years before, I couldn't find any buyers.

I needed some sort of cash flow and needed it BADLY. So guess what? I traded four of the lots into an old run-down complex of rentals consisting of cabins, trailers and a home that was cash flowing about $1,200 per month. That was just what I was in need of.

Then a couple of months later the manager disappeared, stole, as in went south with the entire month's rental receipts. This was the start of the problems. I found another manager, got back on track and got by about a year before the first of Two Big Problems.

The mining company had built fifty or sixty new homes that they were renting to their employees. The price of molybdenum had plummeted and the mine was scaling back big time.

They then put their houses up for sale to their employee/renters with no down payment. Guess where part of my renters went? Right, to buy a no-money down house with payments very little more than their monthly rent.

Now for the Big One! On October 28, 1983 the 7.3 magnitude earthquake hit central Idaho with its epicenter near Mount Borah, Idaho's' highest mountain. The Lost River valley dropped about nine feet and Mount Borah rose about six inches.

The fracture was over twenty six miles long and seven miles deep. Yes, a big one that killed two Challis children, Travis Frank and Tara Leaton.

My rental complex was located at the base of a mountain. Giant rocks the size of small automobiles rolled off the mountain and into the parking lot of the Hillside Apartments and the remaining renters left.

From a positive cash flow of $1200 per month to a negative cash flow of considerably more than that in the space of a few weeks.

I gave up. Gave Don Mann, the guy I had traded with, a deed in lieu of foreclosure, and walked away.

My entire souvenir collection of that period in time is a Hudson's Bay wool blanket and this painting that I held for collateral on unpaid rents. The four free and clear lots I traded in on the apartments were worth about twenty thousand each at that time.

That's the basis for my $80,000 painting. The same lots today according to a release on March 1, 2006 could be worth somewhere around $400,000 each so I guess I might have a $1,600,000 painting!

**THE VALUED PAINTING!**

# Chapter 17

# Interesting Employees of Days Gone By

Through the years of being owners of ranches and outfitting businesses we have employed quite a diverse group of individuals.

Some were very good employees and became good friends – others were not so very good.

**Arlo Lewis -** One of the most memorable. He was a talented, knowledgeable, hard worker and worked for us intermittently for nearly twenty years at the ranch and hunting camps in Nevada and at the Hotzel Ranch and Taylor Ranch Hunting Camps in Idaho.

I first hired him about 1959, at our Angel Creek Ranch in Nevada. I needed a Cat Skinner to pull a landplane, leveling land. I went to Wells and while in The El Rancho Hotel at Waldo Jones and Gene Pengellys' barber shop; I inquired about a possible hand to hire.

They told me to go to the Elite Club and inquire for the whereabouts of one Arlo Lewis. I went in and asked the bartender and was motioned to a game of pool underway in the back of the bar.

This small statured, semi-inebriated, banty rooster type in the eight ball game informed me he was Arlo Lewis. I informed him of my need of a helper for a month. He asked me what it paid. I replied "One hundred twenty five dollars a month."

ARLO LEWIS ABOUT 1970

He drew himself up to his maximum tip-top height of about five foot five inches and said, "Hell, I'm worth twice that much!" "Give me a job at $250 a month and after two weeks if you don't think I'm worth it, the two weeks are FREE!" So, the one month employment stretched, off and on, for nearly twenty years.

His major weakness was an addiction to the "Demon Rum." His favorite saying, "Hell, I'm not a wino, I'll drink

**ARLO'S TREE BY COUGAR DAVES CABIN AT THE TAYLOR RANCH**

anything!"

His second weakness was consistently getting turned around in the mountains. The famous "Lost Guide" ridge was named for Arlo, after he succeeded in a pair of major disorientations of major proportions in the same area!

The first time, with two hunters and a two night lay out. The second, with one hunter for another night out, and this was all within a couple of weeks. (All you other guide types that claim it was named after you – wrong, Arlo was the first!)

He was a great friend, baby-sat our daughter Kay, had a nice singing voice, was a master metal smith and a good cook. He was a caretaker of the Taylor Ranch for the University of Idaho when he passed away.

**Joe Foss and John Lindstrom** - I hired these two together on the Nevada Ranch. They also weren't winos – they also would drink anything!

Joe Foss, having a famous name (Governor of North Dakota, President of the National Rifle Association etc.) Joe was prone to capitalize on it whenever possible as in a free drink at the bar now and then. Somehow, I had sent him to Elko, Nevada in my pickup for parts.

He ran it out of gas along about Deeth. (I found out later he had tarried in Wells to the tune of several drinks.)

A highway patrolman stopped to check on him and Joe in his inebriated condition told the policeman, "No problem officer, I'm just out of gas and Stan is going to land his plane on the highway and bring me some!"

John Lindstrom and Joe Foss were left for a few days at the ranch. They would be working and preparing their own meals in our kitchen. A few days later when Joy and I returned we found they had drank most of the available whiskey and wine and diluted the bottles with water. Until there wasn't much color left and no taste!

John Lindstrom told us he would probably die from falling off a boxcar. Sure enough, a few years after he worked for us we read, in the Elko Daily Free Press, that he was run over by a train, in Elko, either trying to get on or off of one.

**"Bullshit Bob" & "Outhouse Bill" -** These two nicknames probably pretty well describe each individual without much further descriptions.

Bob claimed to be a (along with many other claims), master packer, cutting horse trainer, country western singer just waiting for his big break from Nashville. He dressed all in black just like Johnny Cash but that was pretty much the extent of any further comparisons.

He drew his pay after the first week, went to town and, unbeknownst to me, papered the town with bum checks. I fired him a couple days later for letting the saddle blanket come completely out from under his riding saddle and causing a sore on his horse.

He had only been gone a few days when the people that had cashed his checks because he "worked for Stanley Potts" started calling.

I then found out he had given me and them a phony home address and phony Social Security number. A real dandy! And no telling how many poor saps was or will be taken prior to and after he got to us.

Outhouse Bill, as the nickname implies – whenever you needed something done or needed to know where he was – just holler toward the outhouse.

I'm not sure if he had perpetual diarrhea, constipation or what but he had figured out how to avoid great quantities of work by being "indisposed."

I took him on one extended sheep hunt. He let his riding horse get away with the pack string and rolled the string. One of our best little mules, Pat, ended up with his neck pulled down and basically ruined from the wreck.

Then I left him to watch the stock for a few days while we backpack hunted for a ram. When the hunter and I returned we found he had eaten all the snacks and drank all the beer! Another dandy!

**Ron H.** - Ron was a stout built, young chap that drove clear across two states pleading for a job. No day would be too long, no task to great.

The first day on a pack trip to set up a camp and cut trail, I unpacked the stock in early afternoon and turned them loose to graze in a nice grassy meadow. We had some lunch and I mixed a water bucket full of Tang,© an orange juice mix, so we could re-hydrate and have it for supper and breakfast.

It was hot and my plan was to rest an hour or so and then go on foot, with a crosscut saw and axe to clear trail, up some steep country in the cool of the evening. When I got ready to go my "no task too great – no day too long partner," said he was too tired and needed a few days tc get in shape for this strenuous of work. (We had ridden about ten miles and walked downhill about two.)

"O.K. Ron, just watch the stock and I'll go cut logs out of the trial until dark." That night when I returned, the horses had been in the grub boxes, eaten all the bread, cookies, lettuce and apples and had drank the water bucket full of Tang©!

My great helper had "rested" through the whole commotion. Needless to say his term of employment ended when we got out of the mountains on that trip.

**Wino Wayne -** Wayne was another of life's characters – honest as the day is long and a steady worker. However, he also had a major problem of getting into the "Suds," or any other drink containing alcohol.

He had been a professional boxer of, evidently, some talent. He had at least once, in his pugilistic career, fought a World Champion although evidently not too successfully. He had the old newspaper clippings to verify it.

Always, while under the effects of alcohol, if anyone moved fast arcund him he would go into a boxer's crouch. He would then dance around, shadow boxing and exhaling thru his nose toward the suspected opponent.

Consequently, his drinking partners would encourage and stimulate him to shadow box around while reliving his days in the ring.

During one of his parties at the hunting camps we had several guests and Wayne evidentially took offense to one of them teasing him and showed back up waving his pistol around. We disarmed him which wasn't hard in his condition. However he wouldn't settle down and was making a general pain of himself.

One of our long time hunters, Hy Dustman, took him to his sleeping bag and inserted Wayne headfirst into the bag and zipped him in! That settled Wayne down for the rest of that evening.

I had left Wayne and another helper at the Taylor Ranch to repair tack and care for the horses and mules. Joy and I had flown back to take care of the Nevada Ranch.

In only a few days the other helper, Floyd Posing, radioed out. He said Wayne had broken into Joys and my cabin and had gotten some of our whiskey and was just staying drunk.

I'd had it! It was winter time and I had to fly about four hundred miles up to get him. I took the flying club Super Cub and when I landed I was not in what you would call a "temperate mood."

He was still drunk and I helped him get his gear loaded and strapped him in the rear seat. I decided to give him the airplane ride of his "ever-loving" life.

The Taylor Ranch is located on Lower Big Creek in the very steep central Idaho Mountains. The canyon bottom is very narrow, probably averaging less than one hundred yards wide with bends, cliffs and trees. It's about eight miles of these until it flows into the Middle Fork of the Salmon River drainage that widens out somewhat.

I took off and screamed along just above the treetops and with wingtips sometimes only a few feet from the cliffs. When I got to the Middle Fork I looked back expecting to see a terrified passenger. Wayne had his head down between his knees! I don't think he had ever looked out the window after we had taken off!

**Floyd Posing -** I learned a lot from Floyd. He had packed and guided for several different outfitters both on river trips and horse outfitting operations.

When I first hired him I was pretty green (meaning there was an awful lot about packing, and organizing I need to get a better handle on). He could get a pack string out of camp faster than any helper I've ever had. It took me a year or two of watching and studying his methods before I could do it as fast.

His knowledge really helped me to become a better professional packer in my forty six year career as owner of outfitting businesses.

When Joy and I had our little farm near Mackay (actually old Houston,) between 1954 and 1957 we raised alfalfa hay, seed peas, certified potatoes and certified barley seed. There was usually some crop being raised or cared for in some manner most months of the year.

There was quite a contingent of young aspiring rodeo cowboys that knew "Pottsville" was a possible chance at best, for a few days work to earn enough for entry fees at the next rodeo. At worst, a square meal and maybe a tank of gas could be figured into the equation of "going down the road."

**Avon Young -** An Arizona cowboy, Avon showed up when he was only about fourteen years old and called our place home during the summer rodeo season. He helped out for his board and room and brought a couple of his buddies a summer or two to do the same.

Avon was a very talented bull rider in his younger days and then moved to Fallon, Nevada and became a top steer wrestler.

I'll walk through some of the names I can remember of this period in time.

Starting with, Avon Young and his buddy, fellow Arizonian, Tom Ramsey, who was an excellent calf roper and team roper. Tom won the team roping one year at Tucson teamed up with World Champion Chuck Sheppard. There was also Hector Dailey from Arizona that roped calves and team roped.

Idaho cowboys that usually showed up during haying or thrashing time were mostly saddle and bareback bronc riders and bull riders. This group consisted at different times of Dick Anderson, Larry Robinson, Dick "Dickie" Fenstemaker, Larry "Shep" Hatfield, Bob Tyler, Larry Edmondson and Ronnie Koll.

When we were developing the side roll sprinkler system on our ranch at Clover Valley, Nevada, I'd hired a young cowboy from Ukiah, California, named Joe Aggi.

I had about six quarter mile lines of 40' joints of pipe, wheels between each joint with Farmland© power mowers in the centers, to get set up.

I had a girl crew of school kids including my three girls Kay, Robyn and Stani, and their friends Rini and Suzy Smith. Aggi got to be the foreman. Joy and I had to fly up to the Taylor Ranch for a day. We flew back the next day and I dropped down over the field and all the lines were finished! A super job by the foreman and the all-girl crew.

Joe was a really good steer wrestler. He helped several years at the hunting camp. He had a problem controlling his temper, but was a great helper and good friend. Joy and I flew to California to his and his bride Ilene's wedding.

**Con Hourihan -** He had gotten back from Viet-Nam and was buckarooing for a neighboring ranch in Nevada. I met him one day, after I'd gotten a haircut at the El Rancho Barber Shop. We had a couple of beers and he found I had the hunting camps in Idaho.

Long story short, he helped a month the first year, all season the next few years and then bought our business. Joy and I and our son-in-law Jerry Black helped him a few hunts while he was getting started. This is another top hand.

Interesting side-note, I'd co-signed a car loan for a guy that went bad on it. After a couple years he showed up back in town. He gave me a call, apologized and said he had a bartending job at K G Thompson's Trail Forty Bar and would pay me off at twenty bucks a month. I received two months payments and no more.

Hourihan had come to town, whupped up on him, he got fired, and that ended my chance to recoup! Ah well.

# Chapter 18

## Recent Horse Wrecks

I have been involved in a few horse catastrophes since my last books. As those of you that have read my past books know, horse wrecks and buck offs have played prominently in quite a few stories in the medley of my life.

The two most recent glaring memories, A.K.A. "buck offs," were courtesy of one female equine of blood red, sorrel color, with a big wide white strip in her forehead known appropriately as "Blaze."

Blaze was not the most beautiful creature ever invented. Her head was about the same size as a thirty gallon barrel with ears and her feet would have been right at home on any of the "Budweiser Clydesdales."

She was just a big gentle pussycat until she decided to buck. I had needed some gentle riding horses for the hunting camp and had my son-in-law Jerry Black buying horses for me.

He said this young girl came riding Blaze down the lane bareback and with just a halter on. The price was right and the mare seemed exactly like what I needed - young, big and gentle.

We used her for a year or two with no problems. Put hunters on her, you could catch her anywhere and we even made a bell mare out of her to keep track of the mule string.

If you needed a packhorse she gladly filled the bill. I naturally had to be the one to uncover her dark side (probably better me than one of the hunters). As with most horses that have been "kid broke" she had been allowed to do a lot of things her own way. She did things according to her system and didn't want to change.

I was still recuperating from my fall down the mountain in October of 1999. I had been about seven months healing eleven broken ribs, a punctured lung and both shoulders rebuilt. (See chapter 25, "The Longest Night," in my first book, "The Potts Factor Versus Murphy's Law.")

Buck off number 1: The second shoulder had been operated on about a month before my first set-to with Blaze. I was riding her down my landing strip here at Colson Creek when the Forest Service Trail Crew drove by up on the road about one hundred yards away.

**I'M RIDING JOE (HIS EATING ALONG THE TRAIL CAUSED HIS DEATH) BLAZE NEXT TO LAST AND SPAR LAST IN STRING.**

I wanted to talk to them so waved them to a stop and started riding her up the hill towards them. Blaze decided she didn't want to go up the hill so I over and undered her with the tail of my halter rope. Mistake!

She dropped her head and started to buck going up the hill. I was barely able to stay aboard going up hill and we were coming to the top. I remember thinking, "Boy! If she keeps this up on level ground, I'm gone!"

Sure enough, we got to the hill top and I sailed high in the air. All I could think of as I was tumbling back down toward the earth was to try and not land on my freshly repaired left shoulder. The thought was correct; however the execution left lots to be desired.

Crash! I landed right on the hard rocky road and on the left shoulder.

Jim Upchurch, the trail crew foreman, and some of his crew came running down the road to see how badly wounded I was.

I sat up and gingerly moved my shoulder around. Other than pain from the collision with the hard earth, it felt o.k.

I told Jim, "That Dr. Chandler does a pretty good job of repairing shoulders to withstand that violent a crash!"

Buck off Number Two: This one happened about two years later back in the mountains on a sheep hunt.

Lionel Brightwell from Boise, Idaho had drawn a sheep tag and hired me to outfit and guide him. Lionel was a sucker for punishment as Pat Hendron (another of my guides), and I had succeeded in skunking him when he had drawn a tag a few years prior.

Alan Swanson was working for me as a guide and Holton Quinn was along to provide an extra set of eyes and assistance on the hunt. Holton ultimately found Lionel's ram a few days later.

I had dropped the three of them off on a ridge top and they would hike the rocky rim of the canyon for a few miles. I would take all the stock and we would rendezvous later that afternoon.

I was once again riding the "Blaze." It had been a couple of seasons since my first buck off in the hard road. We'd used her steady with no further problems. She was cured and foolproof again!

"Right?"

"Wrong!"

When my three "companeros" arrived we visited for a few minutes. They had found no rams so we would head back to camp. The hillside where they met me was very steep. It was probably in the neighborhood of seventy degrees steep. Because of the every year or so forest fires back there, every guide must pack a cross cut saw long enough to cut big ponderosa and fir logs that fall over the trail. We took some seven foot crosscut saws and cut through in the center at an angle so they would fit in a rifle scabbard.

We were ready to depart so we pulled the cinches up on all the stock and mounted up. Immediately, Blaze whirled and started bucking straight down the nearly vertical hill!

If you have never looked between the ears of a violently bucking horse going down a steep hillside you have never experienced sheer terror!

I knew if I went off forward the ravens would have a nest built in my drawers before I touched the ground and it wouldn't really matter because I'd be long dead either from the fear of the fall or the rapid deceleration when I hit.

About the third jump there was a loud crack. I had no idea what it was as I was trying to figure how to guarantee a buck off to the most uphill side I could find. Luckily, it worked and I rolled to a halt watching the "resident witch" buck on around the hillside while popping my stirrups over the center of the saddle.

The guys had all heard the big loud crack also. They figured she had broken a leg or it was my neck or back.

When she bucked back to us and stopped, the handle, one-half of my saw, was hanging out of the scabbard. She had somehow hit the ground so hard it had broken the saw in two pieces! The breaking saw was the loud crack.

About here I had somewhat of a brain malfunction. I spun her around, sailed the broken saw out over the canyon, kicked her in the belly and aiming her for some slightly mellower ground, I jumped back on.

She walked off just like an old plug! About then I realized I'd probably thought I was eighteen again instead of sixty eight. I asked Allan if he wanted to lead the way back to camp.

"No," he said, "I've only been here one time with your grandson, Jay Black, and we were lost all the way to camp!"

The next day, (getting some logic back in my brain) I caught my old gentle mule "Doc," we hunted some new country and Lionel got his bighorn ram.

I had purchased a big, young sorrel gelding from Marvin Hansen. The horse had been rounded-up with a mustang gather on the East Fork of the Salmon River and happened to be of better than average breeding and conformation.

One of the canyon names where the horse gathers occur is Spar Canyon. The horse carried a government neck brand and the name "Spar." Marvin had been riding and packing Spar for a year or so and he was fairly well trained, or "broke".

He would buck sometimes if you cinched him too tight too soon after saddling him. This is referred to as a "cinchy" horse in the vernacular of western horseman language.

He would occasionally buck at other times but he had a pretty good "mouth". As in, could be controlled with the bridle reins and spun out of his buck. Also, he couldn't hold a candle to Blaze in the bucking department.

His major problem was in the pack-string. This problem caused lots of wrecks before we got smart enough to let him train us. His problem was his occasional aversion to having stock behind him in the pack-string. This aversion was not all the time but occasionally, under the wrong circumstances, far too often.

My most painful memory (as in a physically painful wreck) happened one morning in the middle of the Salmon River Road about one quarter mile upriver from the Stoddard Pack Bridge. I had packed my string of about eight head here at Colson Creek and headed out.

**SLEEPY, GENTLE BLAZE. HAH! SPAR IN THE CENTER GETTING A DRINK.**

It's about three miles to the Stoddard Trail Head at the mouth of the Middle Fork of the Salmon. There are hitching rails there and it is an excellent place to tighten cinches and do any adjustment of the cargo prior to crossing the pack bridge and heading up into the steep country.

I was traveling alone and had had virtually no problems with either stock or cargo. It was, unfortunately, a prelude to moderate disaster. I'm ambling quietly along the road when all of a sudden a blow up in my string, horses and mules bucking and kicking and trying to go around my riding horse.

In a few moments, some breakaways did what they were supposed to do, and now instead of one pack-string I had three and all of them out of control.

The little strings of two or three went by me and then turned around and headed back towards me. Most of them had settled down but Spar was still bucking and dragging a couple more behind him. I had gotten off my saddle horse and was catching loose stock and trying to get organized when Spar and company crashed into the remainder of the stock.

Things happen far too fast to be able to relate the entire scenario in a situation like this but the ultimately very painful result was this: Spar jumped on my right foot with a new toe and heel calked shoe. He probably weighed twelve or thirteen hundred pounds with the packs on and it felt like all of it was on that stomp on my toe.

The pain was a strong nine on a scale of one to ten! I hobbled around on basically one foot; finished unraveling my lash up and then it was decision time once again. I knew I had at least a broken Big Toe and probably more.

No matter what, the pack-string would have to either be taken back to Colson Creek and unpacked or onto Cradle Creek. It would not rank up there with "Life's Enjoyable Memories" either way.

I opted to continue onward or at least toward, Cradle Creek, eighteen miles to the south. I was just getting back on my saddle horse when a car pulled up headed down river. It stopped and the passenger in the front seat was Senator John Peavey from Hailey and Carey. He asked if they could help and I told him thanks, but I had it under control.

Luckily I had no more problems other than walking three miles down the Big Grassy on my left foot with the right one only for balance. I had hay cubes and grain in my packs so unpacked, unsaddled and put the string in the corral. I knew I would not be able to wrangle on one foot.

Once again, it was major decision time. My shoe where the horseshoe had come down was cut and I could see the bloody sock. The foot was swelled up very tight. I knew if I removed it I would never get the shoe back on. I decided to just loosen the shoe laces, get something to eat, get some kind of rest if I could, then saddle up and head out "dark thirty" to see how badly the foot was hurt.

No problems of major proportions except huge blisters on the left foot from only walking on it and big toe broken near the foot. The other toes were only bruised and black and blue. Lost three toenails but as they say in this part of the world, "it's a long way from my heart!"

Yah! Old hardhead learned to put Spar on the caboose end of the string and solved lots of problems.

**Sometimes it takes them quite awhile to teach me anything!**

# *Chapter 19*

# Recollections of a Horse Trader

When we were in the early years of ranching in Nevada anything that had a chance of generating some much needed "dinero" was studied with great care and diligence.

We had sold and delivered some registered Quarter Horse mares to a gentleman in Los Angeles named Bill Lampkin. Bill had been quite instrumental in the formation of some of the early associations to register and improve the Quarter Horse bloodlines.

We had some Oklahoma Star, Chief McCue and Joe Moore breeding and Bill knew all of their history back to the first one registered. I believe that was Wimpy P-1.

Anyway, Bill liked our mares and offered me a job locating and purchasing good papered mares and delivering them to his ranch at Norco, near Los Angeles.

We become quite good friends over the next couple of years but I found out, not quite as good as I'd thought. Bill belonged to a horsemen's group of quite important and wealthy ranchers, politicians and movie stars. The name I believe was, "The Los Rancheros Visitadores!"

Each summer they would have a one week horseback trip through a part of the California Mountains. Not on the same order as a Potts pack-string but with catered meals, catered bars and western bands, a top of the line celebrity outing.

Each member was allowed one guest and Bill Lampkin invited me! I was for a month or so in what is known as "hog heaven." And then, in what could have been the early stages of the "Potts Factor," I got a phone call from Bill that "burst my bubble," so to speak. It seems Dale Robertson, the western actor, wanted to go on the ride.

Yep! Potts got bumped for a movie star.

I sort of got even a short time later (unintentionally I swear.) We had sold our ranch in Nevada to one of Bill's friends, acquaintances, business associates, or whatever name, K.B. Kiker. (See "The Potts Factor Versus Murphy's Law" page 55 for more.)

Bill had invited us all to dinner at a nice restaurant down on the wharf. He and his girl friend picked Joy and I up at our hotel in his new wine colored Cadillac© that he had picked up that day. During the later stages of the dinner, girl friend and Bill became involved in a rather serious altercation. Serious as in he slapped her and knocked her off her chair.

There was far too much alcohol served and that led to the row. He threw me the keys to his new Caddy, called a cab for he and girlfriend, threw some money at the waiter and disappeared.

I found the car and Joy, I and Kiker got in. Kiker was a little smothered by the "Demon Rum" but insisted on giving me driving directions.

He said "turn here. I want to show you where I just lost five million dollars!"

It was a brand new residential subdivision with homes practically completed and roads that were still only dirt. It had been raining for several days and the roads were mostly under water.

I was quite concerned that the new caddy was not the most proper mode of transportation in a sea of soft mud! Sure enough, in one of the swamps, gravity and slime overpowered the caddy. We opened the doors and muddy water flowed in to seat level!

I left the keys in it and we slogged to solid ground, found a phone booth and called a cab. The next day I called Bill Lampkin and told him where I had parked the caddy. That terminated my friendship and employment with Bill Lampkin.

# Chapter 20

# Of Mountain Horse Tragedies

## Betty's Last Trip

In July of 2001, several of us went on a pack trip to Stoddard Lake. The impetus for the trip was activated by a couple of different events.

First, the Idaho Outfitters and Guides Association held a fundraising banquet called "The Spring Thaw." where different businesses, outfitters, flying services, sporting good stores, hotels etc., donated trips or merchandise to be auctioned.

The money would be used for the day to day operation of the association along with the necessary political maneuvering involving the legislative bodies and management agencies overseeing rivers, forests, and big game populations – all crucial to an outfitter's existence.

Joy and I, through our outfitting business, Stanley Potts Outfitters, donated a one week trip to the auction. Debbie Simonds purchased the trip for her family including husband Grant and sons Greg and Jess.

Grant was the Executive Director of the I.O.G.A. and kept himself updated on the different businesses that make up the diverse membership. Also, at that time, a neighboring outfitter, Bud Lesley, was undergoing cancer treatments and a fundraiser was held in the Salmon Valley for Bud. We donated another trip to help raise funds for his medical expenses.

Jo Ann Carroll and Marcella Hendricks purchased this trip and we coordinated the two trips into one. My helpers would be Alan Swanson and Marvin Hansen.

The trip would involve the enjoyment of a mountain pack trip along with listening and looking for the recently planted Canadian wolves. We would camp at Stoddard Lake for a few days, hike to other lakes and hopefully catch some fish.

We owned a small black mare that was one of the kind you wish they were all like. She was gentle, sure footed, smooth to ride and completely honest. This mare named Betty would be Debbie's mount for the trip.

We had heard wolves howl on the trip (one of those actually howled at the sound of my cross cut saw cutting through a dry lodgepole log). We went to the lake, got snowed on for two days, the fish wouldn't bite but we had a nice campout nevertheless. Heard more wolves and actually saw one on the trip out.

On the last day of the return trip I was in front of the guests when Debbie hollered to me.

"Stan, Betty is walking funny, like she's going to step off the trail."

I told her to walk up to the front and ride my horse Joe and I'd see if I could tell what was wrong with Betty. I went back and Betty's eyelids were fluttering. When she would walk a few steps she would stagger like she was winded.

I told the group to go on ahead with Alan and Marvin and the pack strings. I would follow as best I could walking and leading Betty.

I would lead her a few steps, stop to rest her, and she would go to eating grass along the trail just like nothing was wrong. But then, after only a few steps more her eyelids would go into an involuntary flutter and she would resume staggering.

After about thirty minutes I finally made the last of the uphill trail. Another hundred yards or so and it would be all downhill and mellower terrain. However, this few hundred feet of trail cut around the top of some nearly vertical cliffs.

I rested her for ten or fifteen minutes and then started to lead her around the trail. After only a few steps she staggered and stepped off the lower side of the trail. She could barely hold herself; I un-cinched and unsaddled her as she was still staggering. I wanted to tie the halter rope to something to help her maintain her balance. However, it was too short.

I undid my belt, hooked it over a small vertical rock in the trail and was able to get the halter rope tied off to the belt. About then she fell, exerting full weight on the rope and leather belt. Just a few feet below her was the start of the cliffs.

The next few moments have played back in my mind many times since then like the nightmare it turned into. With all the tension on the halter rope the strands slowly stretched and one by one they frayed and broke. There was nothing I could do but watch the bad movie unfold.

The last strand parted and Betty flew over the cliff to probably certain death. I left my belt and the broken rope along with the saddle and blankets and followed downward the landslide that was developing.

I could not leave without knowing the final outcome. About one thousand feet below lay Betty's mangled and broken body. I could only hope that she had died in the first few moments.

It took me over two hours to climb back up through the cliffs to the trail plus another couple of hours to the main road and the rendezvous with the rest of my group. Jo Ann had come back to see if she could help but had somehow missed the belt and broken rope tied to the rock and the gear below the trail. It was a sad ending to an otherwise fun trip.

I went to Salmon and talked to the veterinarian to see if I could find out what had happened. He said the fluttering of the eyelids indicated probably a heart-attack or stroke. It was something that had cut off the oxygen supply to her brain.

It was heart wrenching to relive this tragedy on the written page but, the best I can do to remember the great little mare Betty. I just wish I had been able to save her.

## Joe

We had sold our outfitting business along with the riding horses, mules and inventory. The new outfitter was trying to get some of the necessary trail work done and had some helpers hired that weren't the most knowledgeable about handling stock in the mountains.

One of them was back by Stoddard Lookout working on trail. His riding horse was another old faithful, Joe. The same that Debbie Simonds rode out in the Betty Chapter. Joe's worst habit was a perceived constant need to graze along the trail.

Riders that were somewhat knowledgeable would keep his head under a little more control. I don't know exactly what happened. The young lad that was riding him brought me Joe's halter and a lock of mane from his foretop.

He reported that Joe stepped off the trail in a bad spot and fell to his death. Another untimely death to a hardworking friend.

# Chapter 21

## Ranching Struggles and Possible New Adventures

About the time we were not able to make the ranch in Nevada pay off (which seemed like most of the time), we were kicking and scratching for an enterprise that might prove successful. We were doing about everything we could think of to generate dollars on a ranch that was in the center of a drought.

We were running a hunting camp, raising and trading horses, running all the cows we could feed and trying to sell or trade the ranch. I was working construction and welding jobs, trying to keep the bills and ranch payments made, but it seemed the noose was slowly tightening.

Joy was driving the mail stage through Clover and Ruby Valleys for John Quillici. It was 160 miles round trip twice a week. In addition to the mail she delivered groceries and equipment parts to the outlying ranches.

The airlines were badly in need of more pilots. I was a private pilot then and they offered a plan to finish your flight training and pay you wages until you built the necessary time to become part of the flight crew.

I was approaching the age that if I made a decision to try, with the airlines, I would have to do it soon. If I remember right, the program was closed as soon as you reached thirty-eight years of age.

We finally decided to keep struggling along and hoping our fortune would change.

One venture that showed some potential would involve a major alteration of our existing lifestyle if it came to pass.

While helping Dirk and Marta Agee move some cattle to new pastures one summer I met a friend of theirs named Vince Mancini, from Salt Lake City, Utah. If I remember correctly he was a nephew of Henry Mancini, the famous composer and musician. Vince would buy weaned cattle and bring them to the Agee's ranch in the O'Neil Basin for summer pasture.

Vince was trying to put an ambitious livestock venture together in Brazil. His plan was the development of cattle ranches and irrigated farms along with a pet food cannery. The location would be near the mouth of the Amazon River.

With cheap land, cheap labor and cattle that were only ten cents on the dollar, compared to the United States, he felt the relative proximity to pet food markets in the United States would be a money maker.

The irrigated farms would grow high protein and carbohydrate filler crops like soybeans and corn to be mixed with the beef from the cattle operation.

He offered me a job to go to Brazil with him if he was able to make it work. It didn't work out for us but would have been a completely different adventure, even for a pair that have tried many different adventures.

# Chapter 22

# Frank Lantz

**FRANK LANTZ**
**A FEW YEARS AFTER MY VISITS WITH HIM**

Many years ago, and over several different hunting trips, I became acquainted with one of Idaho's Legendary Mountain Men.

Frank lived at the mouth of Little Squaw Creek that flows from north to south and is a tributary of the Salmon River. What I am penning here are my recollections of the events and happenings Frank related to me over several different hunting trip visits over several years.

As I have noted through reading the biographies of other persons I have noticed there are usually some discrepancies of what is written and what I remember. With that in mind please be advised, this is what I remember.

In this recollection exact dates aren't important. I have deliberately refrained from studying anything about Frank so as to not cloud what is left of my failing old memory.

For accurate dates, pictures and a different perspective read "River of No Return" by my old friend Johnny Carrey and Cort Conley.

I had killed my first bear at the edge of Frank's orchard in the fall of 1958. I had known Frank casually for a few years and as the years and hunting trips went by we became better friends. He had been in and out of the Salmon River Country working at ranching, mining and logging.

When he first came to the area called Little Squaw Creek, I think, it was in 1923, he said he had walked in. He had come from Montana across the head of the Selway River and down Little Squaw Creek. He came to the area with his total belongings on his back. Included in the belongings was a sour dough start he had brought from West Virginia.

The mouth of Little Squaw Creek is a beautiful alluvial fan of approximately one quarter mile on all sides. It is fairly smooth but with great quantities of rocks from pebble size to automobile size deposited by floodwater rushing down the narrow canyon thru the eons.

He told me that there were two men and a woman living there in a lean-to. They had several horses that grazed the flats and nearby grassy hillsides.

Frank stayed with them a few months and found out some of their history. It seems they were two brothers and a sister. The sister had run afoul of the law in Wyoming for killing her husband with an axe.

The brothers had helped her get away and they had ended up at the place now known as Little Squaw Creek and Lantz's bar.

I have no idea of the circumstances regarding the axe killing or the naming of Little Squaw Creek.

Anyways the three were about ready to depart the area and Frank made them a deal for their, "thieves' interest," and a couple of their horses. I think he said he gave them fifty dollars.

There were no trails that horses could use along the Salmon River back then. The trail system was just getting started. The season was getting towards fall and Frank would need some supplies for winter.

He hiked upriver and somehow made it to the city of Salmon, about eighty miles away. There he purchased food stuffs, traps and lumber. With the lumber he constructed a scow and loaded his supplies. His plan was to float down the river to his "diggins," unload the supplies, dismantle the boat and use the lumber to build a small cabin.

Once again, as in many chapters of life, the plan and the execution of same became separated.

Frank made it through a lot of the rapids but at what is now known as "Gunbarrel" he swamped the boat losing it and nearly all of his supplies.

I asked, "Frank, what did you do then?"

He replied, "What could I do, I walked on down the river with what I had and made it through the winter with practically nothing."

The next year he did the same thing but this time the plan and execution jelled and he made it with everything intact. He started his cabin and outbuildings. The following winter he started a trap line to take advantage of some of the fur that roamed the nearby (and you will see) "far by" mountains!

His trap line extended from the Salmon River to the town of Darby, Montana! This is well over sixty mountain miles.

I have found several of his trap caches through the years. Mostly, they would be number two Victors, for martin, with usually a couple number three or fours for fox, coyote, bobcat and lynx.

They would be tied to a limb of a large tree and against the trunk, usually at a tree that he had notched for a martin set with a small pole running at about a forty five degree angle from the ground and about four to five feet up the tree.

Each cache would contain a dozen or so traps. On his last trip of the winter, back from Darby, he would trip and pull his traps, cache them along his snowshoe trail and they would hang there waiting for his return the following fall. I would bet some are still waiting!

It would take six or seven days each way with (I assume) at least a day or so stopover in Darby or Hamilton.

At least, on one of his excursions he had talked a young lady named Jessie into marrying him and returning to the Salmon River as his bride. Jessie had died before I knew Frank so other than his fond remembrances of her I have practically nothing I can relate.

After the Forest Service trail system, along with the accompanying telephone lines were installed there was some communication (as in telephone visiting) between the back country inhabitants.

Dorothy Taylor from the Taylor Ranch on Big Creek, where Joy and I operated one of our hunting camps, visited regularly with Jessie Lantz by radio. However, Dorothy said they never met in person.

Frank went to work for the Forest Service and constructed or at least helped construct the entire trail system in this part of Idaho.

Frank had guided hunters and a lot of them had given him beautiful expensive rifles.

He hated eagles! Said they killed too many of the baby mountain sheep and goats. Most of the rifles would shoot very straight and very far! It was the rare eagle seen in his neck of the woods. He would show me various rocks on both sides of the river that he had picked off eagles. A goodly portion of these were four or five hundred yards away!

Through the years he, and then later he and Jessie had moved rocks, finished building and built terraced garden plots with ditches to irrigate. They had gardens, berry patches and the greatest orchard around. Also, a beautiful hay meadow pasture.

Some of those apple trees have a red color to the meat and are the best I have ever tasted anytime or anywhere. His hay field had strawberries that had gone wild that were as big as plums!

Frank enjoyed an occasional shot of whiskey. I soon picked up on the fact that by bringing a bottle of good whiskey to Frank, when we would go through on hunting trips, he would ask if we need some apples. The answer always, YES! And a gunny sack of lunch apples would accompany us on our hunt.

Frank had constructed a derrick to stack the winters hay for his horses. He could never figure why we had to go way up in the hills for our hunting. His hunting trips (at least in this chapter of his life) were in the skid range of the derrick.

Shoot an elk or deer, drag it over to the derrick with the horse and lift it up to butcher and cool-out, away from bears, coyotes or other scavengers.

One trip down the river, a boat passed us headed upriver. I waved from the packstring but didn't know who I was waving at. When I got to Frank's he was very upset.

It seems my old cowboy buddy, Mike Isley, had been down hunting. Mike had gotten a toothache and drank all Franks' whiskey, to kill the pain! My whiskey traded for extra apples on that trip!

I would have guessed Frank's age during the years he had lived there at early seventies about then. He had cut all the dry trees anywhere near his cabin for firewood.

It takes lots of wood when you use it all winter to keep warm and all summer to cook with. Frank would go up the creek and find a dry tree, at least one quarter mile by now.

He'd fall the tree, cut it in rounds and split it. Then load one of those old army pack boards with a woodpile of well over one hundred pounds and pack it down to the woodshed, unload and stack it and head back up for another load.

I said, "Frank, when do you rest?"

His reply, "While I'm walking back up for another load!"

Frank may have weighed one hundred twenty five pounds, but no more, and he was all muscle, bone and sinew.

We were walking down the trail toward Dwyer Creek one day when he said, "See that Elderberry bush?" "I'll tell you a story about it." All the river boatmen would bring Franks supplies downriver just as a neighborly gesture to the old man.

They would usually pack it up the quarter mile to the cabin or if it was heavy loads – come tell him and have a cup of coffee and a piece of pie with sourdough crust as their reward.

One boatman, Austin Smothers that had a place upstream had evidently had a busy day. He just tossed Franks supplies out on the sandbar and didn't even let Frank know they were there.

When Frank found them they were water dampened and not in good shape. This festered on Frank for quite awhile and then one day, they met on the trail by the elderberry bush.

Frank mentioned the supply incident, probably in not too friendly a manner, Smothers lipped off some reply and Frank had a reply of his own, a right cross. That landed one boatman in one elderberry bush!

Frank was reliving it with a relish! He said, "Every time he'd crawl out I'd hit him again!" Ah! If only the rocks, and that elderberry bush could talk!

Frank's cabin and outbuildings burnt down a few years later. He had sold the property to the United States Forest Service but had retained a lifetime tenancy.

A group of Frank's friends along with the Forest Service built him a new cabin and he remained there for the rest of his days.

## The Feud With Johnny Briggs

It seems quite common for people that live in isolation, or at least semi-isolation, to develop grudges and animosity toward one another. I have witnessed it first hand and read about it also. Quite a large percentage of these "not seeing eye to eye" situations end up in bloodshed.

One of these pockets of mutual resentment involved Frank and his closest neighbor, known as Johnny Briggs, who lived about one half mile upriver, at Fawn Creek, no other year-around neighbors within twenty miles.

What the problem was, I never did figure out for sure. All I know is it was severe enough that neither one of them would walk the trail in front of the others cabin.

They may have both forgotten the original problem but neither had forgotten that they didn't like one another. When I would ask either one about the other the responses were identical and very short. "That crazy S.O.B.!"

I don't know if Johnny was crazy but he was definitely different. My initial encounter with him left great quantities of apprehension in my mind. (As in scared the "peawallopin crap" out of me!)

Picture the following scenario, a very cold, late November day, six inches of snow on the ground. A brisk wind of at least twenty miles per hour, temperatures very little above zero. A very cold young man leading a string of mules downriver into the wind followed by three mounted riders. The young man dressed in all the clothes he owned with one of those army surplus, green overcoats with the parka of wolf or wolverine fur pulled tightly around his face.

For an hour or so prior to the young mans, (me) confrontation with Johnny Briggs I could hear sounds carried by the wind that kept sounding more and more like hounds baying. Finally I was sure it was.

I came into a small, flat, opening of an acre or two. Set back against the hillside to the north was a nearly new cabin constructed of probably two-feet-in-diameter yellow pine logs. I think it was only four logs high.

Smoke curled from the chimney, about a half dozen dog houses surrounded the cabin, each with its own chained howling lion hound.

A two wire fence made of telephone wire encircles the compound with a small wooden gate opening onto the Forest Service Trail that we were traveling along. The fence paralleled the trail with about three feet of clearance, barely enough for the packs on my mules to clear.

In the doorway of the cabin about fifty feet away stood a man with his sleeves rolled up with fresh looking blood clean up to his elbows. Cradled in his arms was a lever action rifle.

About the time the trail reached his fence line the man in the doorway walked down the path to the gate, opened it, stepped to the center of the trail, and turned to face me.

I wished for some major disappearing powder but having none rode up to him, said hello, and stopped.

He didn't say hello. His exact words were "What the hell is this? The whole damn Game Department?" (Amazing how you can remember something this traumatic, exactly, from fifty plus years ago but can't remember what you had for supper last night!)

I told him "No, we're just going down river elk hunting." The next few moments passed very, very slowly.

He then stepped back into his gateway and said "Well, if you ARE the Game Department just keep moving right on down the trail!"

Man, we did and the only thing good I could think of right then was "At least I'm not a Game Warden!" I found out from Frank and the real Game Warden, Mike Wilkins, as they say, "The rest of the story."

For several years there had been a bounty of fifty dollars each on mountain lions. Johnny had been able to take twenty or thirty lions each year. However, the bounty had been revoked and now Johnny was waiting around for the bounty to be re-enacted.

He was killing game to feed his dogs and I think had just killed a mountain sheep the morning of my, "to say the least", exciting encounter.

Mike Wilkins, the legendary Idaho Game Warden, told me two stories about Johnny. The first from many years prior was Mike's first encounter with Johnny (sometimes known also I think as "Johnny Behind The Rocks").

Mike was going down the river on a boat patrol trip when he saw someone coming backwards down some steep cliffs. They pulled the boat in and Mike walked up to visit (as in check out) the person.

It was late in the fall, cold weather time. The guy had on denim overalls and an unlined denim jacket. Over his shoulders was a burlap sack tied with a small cord. In the sack was a gallon of coal oil, a small sack of flour, some coffee, dry beans, a box of matches and some salt.

Against the base of the cliff were a few logs leaned against the cliff known as a lean-to. Very little else but that would be his survival supplies going into the winter. This was somewhere down river from Lantz Bar. I'm not sure where the second story was, only a year or two prior to my first exciting "visit" with Johnny.

Wilkins was on another late boat patrol headed down river several miles below the Horse Creek pack bridge. (It's no longer there except for the concrete abutments between Horse Creek on the north side and Butts Creek on the south.)

On the south side of the river below any trails by several miles was a trapper taking an otter out of a trap. Mike pulled in once more. The trapper was Johnny. Mike asked to see his trapper's license. Johnny replied. "I am afraid I will lose it so I leave it in my car at the end of the road." (In those days, about six miles upstream from the Horse Creek bridge.)

Mike told him, "We have to go down river and we'll pick you up on the way back so I can look at your license."

Mike said he was downriver a couple hours and on the way back up kept watching for Johnny. No sign of him. Mike went under the Horse Creek Bridge and watched the trail to the end of the road above the Salmon River Lodge.

Johnny's car was gone! Mike went upriver in his pickup to Shoup. There was Johnny's car.

Johnny had trotted eight or ten miles, several with no trail, to his car and raced upriver to Shoup and purchased a hot new trappers license to get semi-legal!

I'm not sure what finally happened to Johnny but with the bounty on lions gone and fur prices being down he left the Salmon River. I heard once he was working on a ranch below Mackay for Reed Neilson. Then later, heard he was killed in a logging accident.

Back to Frank Lantz stories, Joy reminded me of both of the next stories. The first was his grizzly bear encounters.

Frank said he had killed three grizzly bears down there each because he had to. Two were surprise encounters where the bears charged him, but one came clear across a canyon several hundred yards.

Franks rifle for his hunting away from the house was a beautiful 250/3000 Savage – not the greatest grizzly rifle ever manufactured but only weighing five pounds or less and easy to pack while hiking or snowshoeing.

The second involved a couple cow elk, his dog and his hunting knife. Frank had a huge scar starting at his wrist and ending about his elbow in the lower biceps.

It seems he was up the canyon a ways and had shot a cow elk at the base of a cliff, but still on the hillside. He was bent over cleaning her when his dog started to growl while looking up the hill.

Another cow had walked out and was looking over the cliff. Franks rifle was right there and he shot the second cow in the head. She fell and came rolling right down to Frank, the dog, and the first elk. She was still somewhat alive and Frank grabbed her around the neck as she rolled by and he hung on.

He had his knife in hand and said every time he was on top he would take a swipe to cut her throat. The end result at the bottom of the hill - cow with throat cut and hunter with arm nearly cut off!

All alone and eighty miles from town, he pressure bandaged it to stop the blood flow and somehow didn't get any infection. Franks beautiful white scar over an inch wide and over a foot long ends this part of the story.

## Frank's Stoddard Creek Sheep Survey

After Frank had worked for the Forest Service for many years, building trails or telephone lines, they had him do some big game surveys.

The one I particularly remember involved them sending him to Stoddard Creek to find out the status of the bighorn sheep population.

I'm not sure on the date but think it was the year I was born, 1934. What I am sure of was what he told me about his report on the sheep in Stoddard Creek.

There are several places in there where you can sit and view a mile or two in several directions. I wish I knew exactly where he sat, not that it makes any difference about this story but only to allow me to visualize it exactly as Frank did.

He told me there were so many sheep in sight that he could not get an accurate count! He would count a bunch, then more would come over a ridge, some would disappear, or a whole new bunch would materialize behind where he had already counted!

His final tally was well over four hundred bighorn sheep in sight at one time! Can you imagine how exciting that must have been!?

## Frank Moran

Many years ago a camp cook of great talent named Frank Moran worked for outfitter Ken Smith, in what was then called the Idaho Primitive area.

At the end of the hunting season most outfitters would be buckling up their camps and moving out of the mountains at about the same time.

Some years Ken Smith's crew including Frank Moran would end up back at the little western town of Challis, Idaho at the same time as Joy and I and our crew. Usually both groups of guides, camp cooks, outfitters and last hunt hunters would sort of requisition the entire facility of one of the local restaurants or bars.

Frank would usually buy several bottles of wine to compliment the meals. The wine and wild stories would flow with equal and ever increasing zeal.

Joy remembers her and Frank having their yearly dance with their hunting pacs as their dancing shoes!

Some of you have heard of or at least knew something about the notorious gangster, "Bugs Moran." "Bugs" was Frank's brother. They were a product of the wild side of Chicago in about the 1920's.

Frank told us he had gotten aimed in the wrong direction also. He remembered as a young lad being paid fifty or one hundred dollars for doing nothing except delivering small packages or brown paper bags a few blocks.

These packages and bags probably contained high dollar payoffs for both the bootleg whiskey and the "protection" money necessary for Chicago businesses to stay in operation during that era.

On February 14, 1929 (St. Valentines Day) at 2122 North Clark Street at a warehouse building known as the S-M-C Cartage Company, owned or leased by, "Bugs" Moran, happened the most famous gangland massacre in history.

Al Capone and "Bugs Moran were competitors and the city's most famous ("or infamous") gangsters at least of the 1920 era.

At shortly after 10:30am that morning at least five men, some of them in police uniforms got out of a police car, entered the warehouse, stood everyone inside against a brick wall and sprayed them with machine gun fire.

Bugs Moran was a few minutes late to meet his men and send two empty trucks to Detroit for bootleg whiskey. His tardiness saved his life as all seven men inside were killed.

Al Capone was eventually targeted as being behind the killings and it started the decline of his criminal empire.

I'm not sure if Frank had left Chicago prior or after this event but he spent the balance of his life in the west away from the gangster life and influence. He lived in Kooskia, Idaho when not cooking at hunting camps in the back country.

# Chapter 23

# Val Goodman

## Living in Three Centuries

Not too many people live to be one hundred years old or older. Far, far, fewer do it in a time period that spans all of one century and in parts of two others.

This amazing chronology highlights a lady that I knew quite well during the last two thirds of that life.

I have gleaned a major portion of world events that transpired during her lifetime from articles in her hometown newspaper, "The Arco Advertiser."

I wish to thank the Arco Advertiser for allowing me to use portions of their articles and think they will add immensely to this story. I will insert most of these events and dates after I formulate and pen my own memories of Val.

Valera Dickson was born January 7, 1899 in Woodruff, Utah. Her parents were Albert and Ellen Dickson. Her father was the sheriff of Rich County, Utah and only a few months after Val was born arrested Butch Cassidy for stealing horses.

The family moved to Idaho where her father leased farms and ranches and worked as a miner at the White Knob mine in Mackay.

Val's first husband was my maternal grandmother, Ada Evans Gray's brother, Urban Evans. Three sons were born to the couple, Bob born October 19, 1920, Jack born April 26, 1923 and Keith on July 5, 1926.

Bob lives in Hemet, California and was kind enough to let me use some of his material including much needed pictures for this story. Keith lives in Boulder, Montana and is still in the ranching business. Jack is deceased.

My first memories of Val were after her and "Uncle Erb" were divorced and she was remarried to Frank Goodman. She was a member of the Atom Buster Riding Club and performed during rodeos and fairs throughout Central Idaho on her favorite mare "Sierra Sue."

Later, after Joy and I were married we square danced in Arco usually one week and Mackay the next. Val was a member of the Arco club and loved to square dance.

After Joy's mother, Marion Blume, was in the Lost River Living Center in Arco we would visit her and Val who had been there since July of 2001.

In her early days there she told me. "I'm not supposed to be here. I walked up the hill to visit, fell and hurt myself and they have made me stay here ever since!"

At one hundred and two years young and not thrilled with extra care is pretty phenomenal! When we'd be visiting she would delight in telling everyone within earshot, "I used to paddle his butt"! "He was an ornery little devil!"

I can't imagine this being correct but – what the heck – it's her story! In her last year or so at one hundred and four years she became pretty feeble and most of the time would be asleep when we'd stop to visit. The strong old heart quit beating on March 30, 2003. My tribute to one of Idaho's true pioneers!

## Events of Interest During Val's Life

Val was born nine years after Idaho Statehood. She was around for the election of 19 Presidents of the United States of America from William McKinley to George W Bush! In order they are: William McKinley, Theodore Roosevelt, William Taft, Woodrow Wilson, Warren Harding, Calvin Coolidge, Herbert Hoover, Franklin D Roosevelt, Harry Truman, Dwight Eisenhower, John Kennedy, Lyndon Johnson, Richard Nixon, Gerald Ford, Jimmy Carter, Ronald Reagan, George Bush, Bill Clinton and George W Bush.

There have been forty three Presidents from George Washington until the present and Val was around for nearly one half of them! Is this History or what!! Also

1) 1901 the First Radio Broadcast.
2) 1901 President McKinley assassinated.
3) 1903 Wright Brothers first powered airplane flight.
4) 1905 Theory of Relativity published.
5) 1906 the San Francisco Earthquake.
6) 1908 Henry Fords Model T automobile.
7) 1914 World War I.
8) 1915 Gandhi opposes Britain with civil disobedience.
9) 1917 Russian Revolution.
10) 1924 Craters of the Moon National Monument established.
11) 1928 First Television Broadcast.

12) 1929 Start of the Great Depression.
13) 1933 the Holocaust.
14) 1934 Social Security established.
15) 1939 World War II
16) 1942 First Nuclear Chain Reaction.
17) 1945 First Atomic Bomb Dropped.
18) 1945 First Computers unveiled.
19) 1945 United Nations formed with great hopes for the future of the earth.
20) 1947 First transistor invented.
21) 1950 Korean War.
22) 1955 Arco, Idaho first city in the world lighted by Atomic Power.
23) 1957 Vietnam War.
24) 1958 Microchips invented.
25) 1961 First man in space.
26) 1961 Berlin Wall erected.
27) 1962 Cuban Missile Crisis.
28) 1963 President John Kennedy assassinated.
29) 1964 Civil Rights movement starts.
30) 1968 Martin Luther King assassinated.
31) 1969 First landing on the moon.
32) 1969 Creation of the Internet
33) 1974 President Nixon resigns from the scandal of Watergate.
34) 1989 The fall of the Berlin Wall.
35) 1990 The Hubble Telescope is in operation.
36) 1991 Soviet Union dissolves.
37) 1991 The Persian Gulf War.
38) 2001 September 11, terrorists destroy the World Trade Center.

My mother, Sarah Gray Potts, and Val were great friends throughout their lives. Two Great Ladies!

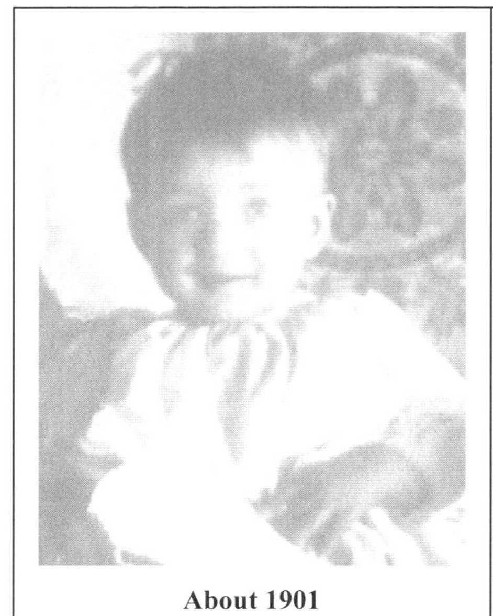
**About 1901**

**1918**

**1998**

**BEAUTIFUL LADY WITH BEAUTIFUL CAR!**

Val's sister Enid Burstedt of Challis wrote the following poem for her sister's birthday celebration:

Today is my sister's Birthday,
She is my friend, my pal.
Her given name is Valeria,
But most folks call her Val.
You might read in any history book,
A story like her life.
Of her pioneering spirit,
Of her Hardships and Strife.
But when adversity would raise its ugly head,
She took it like a man.
She looked the devil in the eye,
And said, "Come get me if you think you can."
In some things scholastic she may not be a whiz,
But when it comes to honesty
She tells it like it is.
And when it comes to handiwork
She leaves me in the shade.
I'd like to have a dollar for each thing,
Those busy hands have made.
She has a heart as big as all outdoors,
And her love is tried and true.
She loves her friends; she loved "old Mike,"
And she loved her horse "Sierra Sue."
She has climbed each mountain to the top
She waded every stream
She has walked each pathway to the end.
Following her dream. Yes, she has traveled many roads,
She set her sprit free, and I can never count
The many things she has done for me,
So happy birthday sister Val,
And here's to many more.
May God go with you all the way,
And make each day happier, kinder
Than was the day before.

Val Goodman, seated, at Monday's party in honor of her 103rd birthday at Lost Rivers Living Center. Standing with Val are, from left, her son and wife, Keith and Carol Evans of Boulder, Montana, and at right, Val's sister and husband, Enid and Frank Burstedt of Challis.

# *Chapter 24*

## Tree Farming

In 1995, Joy and I purchased about twelve acres of land here at Colson Creek. The land was sort of the nucleus of an old homestead that had about sixty five acres originally.

The perimeter along the Salmon River had been subdivided into small home sites in prior years.

There is very little deeded land between North Fork and the Middle Fork of the Salmon River. We figured there would be a market for home sites. We subdivided the acreage into one acre home sites on both sides of an existing 1000 foot landing field.

We sold three of the lots the first year and then it seemed like we couldn't give one away.

The second year we never sold a single one. Not even any serious inquiries. Not having any idea of what the future market for building lots would be we kicked around several ideas of what to try.

The land was too expensive to just sit there. In 1997 we finally decided to experiment with planting one acre to Blue Spruce trees for landscape and Christmas trees if we could grow them.

The land was not fenced and is surrounded by a fairly heavy concentration of mountain creatures as in deer and elk and Mountain Sheep.

We had no idea if the trees would be eaten, stomped out or what. The little trees were only six inches high.

We found the trees were most susceptible to damage the first winter. With a few inches of green sticking out of the snow, some of the tops were eaten off then but by the second or third year – Blue Spruce needles become pretty sharp and damage from grazing becomes minimal.

However, we found the bull elk, buck deer and mountain sheep rams would walk by thousands of trees out in the surrounding forest just to work the velvet from their horns or scratch the ticks from between their horns on our baby tree plot.

It appeared from our first years experiment with five hundred trees to have some potential so each year we would plant from five hundred to one thousand trees until we had trees of various sizes growing on most of the remaining lots.

There was still no visible market for home sites for the next several years.

For some reason in 2005, people started to realize that if they wanted a place to build a home down here, with good steelhead fishing, river running, and surrounded by big game hunting, they better get serious.

We sold most of the remaining lots and retained the use of the land from three to five years to harvest the trees for landscaping. It appears there will be some type of market for landscaping trees but not Christmas trees. We are just too far away from any population center to market Christmas trees.

The next few years will show if we made a good call, (possible allergy.) One possible problem cropped up during our initial harvesting process in 2005.

I spent about three weeks digging, potting and balling & burlapping trees and then hauling them to Salmon and planting them.

There is lots of contact with the limbs and needles during the process. Midway through the harvesting I broke out with a severe itching rash on my back.

The doctors got it under control with salve and medications but could not tell me the cause. One leaned toward calling it a possible allergy to blue spruce! I guess we will find this out also. We have purchased a new tree spade and John Deere Skid Steer and will be moving our trees to new homes.

SOME OF THE LARGER TREES IN 2005

WHAT THEY HAD LOOKED LIKE EIGHT YEARS PREVIOUS

SHADOW SURVEYS HIS TREE FARM

A COUPLE ACRES OF THE TREES

# Chapter 25

## Life Flight Number Two

You may remember, if you read my second book, **"Look Down on the Stars,"** that I had catapulted my "kit thing" airplane into the Salmon River and received another Life Flight. NO, the life flight was from a totally unrelated circumstance.

It stemmed from something (we aren't exactly sure), that occurred on a sheep hunt with Brian Edgerton in the fall of 2001.

Holton Quinn was helping me and we had been hunting several days with no luck.

We had finally found a ram for Brian and he was able to make his shots count and got the ram just before dark one cold October evening.

No problems, except that our pack-frames with sleeping bags, extra clothes, food and water are on top of the mountain and we are near the bottom.

There had been no moisture for several weeks and the forest, although fire-scarred from fires the previous summer were extremely dry. We decided that to build any kind of fire would be very risky.

There was a vertical cliff wall across the rocky gulch from where we had caped (skinned) and boned the meat from the ram to allow it to cool and dehydrate for the trip up the mountain the following day.

Brian, Holton and I each built a little nest in the dirt and ashes against the cliff wall and protected from the wind as best we could.

Sleep, at least for me, was out of the question. I was just too cold. I kept tucking my legs and arms to get my entire body under my medium weight jacket but there was always too much Stan hanging out in the cold air. Because of the dry, fire-danger conditions all around us, I had not gathered any wood for a fire for warmth.

Now, about midnight or so, I knew I could not make it through the rest of the night without some warmth. My worry, a few hours previous, of starting a forest fire seemed insignificant now.

I didn't know how Brian and Holton were making out because each of our little dirt/ash nests were out of sight of each other.

I turned my flashlight on and went scrounging fire material. It turned out, whatever kind of wood I found, was absolutely the worst I could have collected.

I rocked in a fireplace about a foot square with cliff wall as one side. I then started a tiny fire of three or four inches across inside my fireplace. AH! Pure ecstasy. About then, I heard movement from the direction Holt had migrated to build his evening's nest. He had seen the firelight flickering on the cliff face and also cherished a little warmth.

At about this stage of the warm up we realized our tiny fire was casting fiery embers into the night sky and nearby dry grass and brush! We both hunkered against the cliff with the tiny fire below us that was casting embers and lighting the nearby area similar to a 4th of July fireworks display, minus the sound. What kind of wood was it? I don't know but not the kind for a safe fire.

About dawn, Brian showed up to enjoy our warmth and help us watch for any ember that might land and start a big fire. We had no water, even to drink, so stomping a fire out as soon as it started would be our only chance.

As soon as we could see to move around we covered our little fire and fireplace with dirt. We then split our loads of sheep meat,

**HOLTON QUINN AND STAN POTTS COLLECTING WATER FROM CLIFFSIDE SEEP INTO ZIPLOC© BAGS AFTER OUR NITE IN THE BEDS OF ASHES AND TWO DAYS BEFORE LIFE FLIGHT NUMBER 2.**

horns and cape, etc. equally and headed up the mountain to our pack frames. We even found a tiny seep of water to quench our thirst on the way up.

At the pack frames we cooked up a big "Mountain House"© breakfast, mixed up great quantities of Crystal Lite© with the water Holton had packed up. He packed at least three gallons about four miles with at least a three thousand foot climb, in addition to carrying his own already loaded pack frame. An additional twenty five to thirty pounds! Thanks, Holton!

It was now looking like a snowstorm would be upon us in the next few hours and we had some very "ouchy" terrain to descend. With no snow on the rocks and slick grass it was a nightmare. If it snowed it would become nearly suicidal!

We lucked out. Descended down out of the bad country and camped for that night. Even if it snowed now we could make it on to the river o.k.

We did, boated across the river and returned to my house. A hot shower and goodbyes to Brian and Holton and I went to bed feeling great. We'd conquered another mountain!

During the night I awoke with severe chest pains. I told Joy I thought we'd better go in for a checkup as this was different than the ordinary aches and pains.

We drove the sixty miles to town and found Dr. Mark Myers once again to try and find out my problem. (Dr. Myers had been in the emergency room two years prior, nearly to the day, when I was life flighted out of the mountains with all the ribs but one on my right side broken, plus a punctured lung and torn up shoulders.)

He started all the testing and did an E.K.G. When the E.K.G. printed out Dr. Myers did not like whatever he saw on it. He faxed and e-mailed a copy to Dr. Stan Wilson, a heart specialist in Missoula, Montana. They concluded that I should get to Missoula A.S.A.P.

I felt very good now. No pain in chest or arms or anywhere. When they loaded me on the plane with oxygen, tubes, monitors attached all over and a nurse keeping track of everything I felt like a wimp.

They unloaded me into the ambulance in Missoula and drove me to Saint Patrick's Hospital full bore. A beautiful red sports car convertible met the ambulance and Dr. Stanley Wilson had a hand on the gurney as they wheeled me in.

It seemed that all the receptionists and nurses in that end of the hospital had their eyes on the gurney. Maybe that is natural but it surely had my undivided attention.

I signed the necessary waivers to insert the stint in the femoral artery for whatever they need to insert to check out your heart. I was lying there watching the graphs on the monitor. My knowledge all gleamed from Dr. Kildare and General Hospital! I thought, "Hell, looks good to me!"

Dr. Wilson had his back to me and watched the monitor for what seemed to me, a long time. Then he turned to me with a big grin on his face. I think his exact words were; "We don't know what is wrong with you, but it isn't your heart!"

Joy and older daughter Kay were driving up. The hospital kept me there a day or two and then Joy and Kay drove me home. All I can lay the chest pain to was my laying on the cold ground for so long. My grandmother Gray used to have chest pains and called it "pleurisy" or something like that.

I think with my lung being weakened pretty badly a couple years before, that I just got some kind of congestion in it.

What made the E.K.G. reading bad – no one knew. Dr. Myers said he had only seen one like it before. Anyway, now you know the story of "Life Flight Number Two."

# Chapter 26

# Aunt Minni

Your first thought when you see the title to this chapter is, "No, I don't need to waste my time reading about somebody's aunt!"

Well maybe you don't, but if you do read it you will find a very interesting mix of early Idaho history – suspense – tragedy and "Stick-to-it-ivness" beyond belief.

Minni Blume Zilkey Carr was my wife Joy Blume Potts' great aunt and Joy's paternal grandfather's sister. Joy and I would stay with her in Winnemucca, Nevada when we would go there each Labor Day for the rodeo or when her son Bud and she would stockpile bum lambs that our daughter Kay and I would go get, a station wagon load at a time.

Most of this story is oral history directly from her lips. She was born in Minnesota about 1884 and maybe in the town of Mankato.

One of her first memories was of falling out of her swing and knocking herself out just as a group of horseback riders went by. She remembers when she woke up that this nice cowboy was holding her and giving her candy but that her family was standing way back away from her.

In later years they told her who the "nice cowboy" was. It was COLE YOUNGER, of the infamous "Dalton Gang" that made their living robbing banks and trains.

She married Bob Zilkey when she was fourteen years old and they had four little boys. Bud (Willard), was a twin to Wickes and the only one I knew. His twin, Wickes, was killed in France in World War One. The oldest boy's name was Frank.

Somehow they had migrated west in a wagon pulled by two horses, at least one of which was a mare with a colt.

They arrived at a small abandoned log cabin with a sod roof about ten miles up Morgan Creek. Morgan Creek drains into the Main Salmon River some ten miles north of and down river from Challis, Idaho.

It was late fall and Minni's husband took the one horse and told the family he was going to Challis to find work. He left them with very little in the way of food or supplies. A few days after her husband rode off to find a job the family had some interesting visitors.

Minni said it was a warm October afternoon and she had the cabin door open. Suddenly a shadow fell over the room. She looked towards the doorway and there stood three Indian men. The men were not looking at her but at the whiskey bottle full of syrup on the table.

One of them asked her, "Where is your man?"

**BOB ZILKEY AND HIS FOURTEEN YEAR OLD BRIDE, MINNI**

Knowing full well if she told him her husband was gone there could be serious trouble she said, “He’s gone a little way to get the horses and will be right back.”

The men went back to their horses and headed up Morgan Creek evidently toward the Salmon River to winter. About an hour later an Indian woman with a newborn baby passed by. She had stopped to have her baby and was following them along the trail.

Winter came and the husband Bob did not return. The food supplies dwindled to practically nothing. One night a mountain lion was around the house and actually jumped and left tracks on the snow covered roof.

Minni had a pistol of some sort and a few shells. One morning not long after the lion visitor the boys were out scavenging for dry berries, watercress, anything for food.

Minni heard a blood-curdling scream from down the creek. She grabbed her pistol and ran a few hundred yards fully expecting the worst. There sat Bud pointing under a bush. “Mom, It’s a rabbit!” With the first fresh meat all winter, supper was a tiny bit brighter that cold Idaho winter evening.

As spring was arriving Minni decided she had to do something. She decided if she could somehow snare or catch the colt, which was now about a yearling, tie him alongside the mother and get the far too big harness from the horse of the unreturned husband and with some training and luck she could hook them to the wagon.

However, with the circumstances being what they were – one hungry lady – four hungry little boys with the oldest only about eight, no food of any kind left and not wanting to shoot the colt for meat, the training program for the colt and all concerned just jelled into action for the attempted trip.

Minni got the tongue of the wagon up to the trunk of a tree. She tied the mare to the tree on one side of the wagon tongue and harnessed her. Then they were able to somehow catch the colt and get the harness on and the straps shortened as best she could.

She got the tongue up between them, the neck yoke hooked and the colt tied to the mother. Then the tugs were hooked and the three smallest boys laid down in the wagon box, smallest boy at the rear with the end gate out of the wagon.

Minni got the reins and the plan was that Frank; the oldest boy, would untie the mare and jump in the wagon in front of the other boys.

If everything went bad and she could see an unavoidable wreck materializing she would yell and each boy would roll out the back with Frank going out last.

Minni got the makeshift team headed in the right direction but couldn't slow them down. They were at a dead run (any of you people that have been involved in a runaway kind of know how it is), and you can bet it was noisy. All runaways are.

Somehow they stayed in the road around the hillsides but when they were nearly to the Salmon River the colt dropped dead from exhaustion.

How they got on to Challis, I'm not sure. On better, leveler terrain the mare may have pulled the wagon alone. Maybe someone helped them.

However, when they arrived in Challis she found the long gone husband alive and well – and living with another woman!

He had just flat out abandoned them. I've often wondered that with the pistol she might have put him down but probably realized he wasn't worth wasting a bullet on.

Minni found work and a place to live and as the boys got bigger they were able to get some schooling and small jobs to help out.

Bud and Wilkes went into Loon Creek when they were a little older and worked for Mr. Falconberry. Bud became an expert horseman and very talented saddle bronc rider from his work and practice with Mr. Falconberry's horses.

He would come out and compete in the early day rodeos and some of the old oval frame pictures I have seen of him in competition are awesome.

He and I and Joy's dad, Lloyd Blume, came up from Nevada in 1958 on an elk hunt so I got to hear lots of stories from his angle. Funniest one was a 4th of July in Challis.

Bud had ridden one of the fairly salty horses he was breaking out from the Falconberry Ranch on Loon Creek to the big Challis Rodeo and celebration. He was riding in the parade down Main Street. All the businesses had awnings or balconies out over the boardwalks. Bud saw a pretty girl he wanted to impress so he put the spurs to his horse to get him to buck and was fanning the horse with his hat and hopefully, making points with the girl.

The next recollection he had was several days later when he woke up under medical care. They said the horse bucked under a balcony and cracked Buds' head on a big wooden beam – no idea who ended up with the girl. So much for trying to impress a girl, I've seen it work in a similar manner myself.

You (possible) readers from the central Idaho area will appreciate this part of the story.

Mr. Falconberry was getting up in years – needed someone to take over the ranch and associated work. He had about seventy-five cows and half that many horses. He told Bud if he would take care of the ranch and the old man until he died, Bud could have it all. Bud turned it down! Too far from the neon lights, rodeos, and oh, yeah! GIRLS!

A few years back when I was a real estate broker, and Dr. Hatch owned the ranch, I had it listed for awhile for $2,000,000. I flew Bob Bloomfield and a group from Sun Valley into look at it but they didn't buy it.

A year later the Forest Service bought it, burned the buildings, and moved out the equipment and is letting it go back to nature.

Anyway, Minni got a divorce from Zilkey and later married a mining engineer that was evidentially fairly wealthy. I think his name was Jack Carr. She told of his buying one of the first automobiles ever in Idaho – prior to any automobile roads.

The method of travel was to follow the wagon roads. They decided to take a little trip to St. Louis on a visiting trip. It took them thirty days to get there!

One especially exciting part of the trip happened somewhere after they got out into level terrain, probably Kansas or Oklahoma. She indicated that a speed of around five miles per hour had been top speed until then.

Now, they had good wagon roads, level terrain, smooth sailing in their modernistic prairie schooner!

Her husband opened it up and they were zooming along at possibly fifteen or twenty miles per hour. Just guessing here but pretty fast!

All of a sudden their nice smooth road went over into a ravine or canyon and the brakes wouldn't stop it! Over the edge and into a tree with accompanying deceleration! Evidently no big hurts but now the spring (remember, the pictures of early cars in museums that had the springs attached to the frame and extending about a foot in front of everything?) is embedded in the tree! This is a completely different method of being stuck.

Finally, a freight wagon came along and hooked a team on the back end and released them from the tree to continue on their venture.

She had some children with Mr. Carr. One, I think, named or called Young Jack Carr. He was a bomber pilot and shot down and killed in Europe in World War Two. Minni had his picture in uniform on her mantle.

After Mr. Carr died she lived with her brother Julius, in Winnemucca next door to her son Bud and wife Frances and son Laddy and daughter Lauralee.

She passed away at the age of (we think), ninety-six. Another Grand Old Pioneer that I had the privilege of knowing.

# Chapter 27

## My Induction into "Idaho Legends of Rodeo/Cowboy Hall of Fame"

Working cattle is a way of life in Idaho's Lost River Valley, it is today as it was years ago. So it was only natural that I started practicing roping everything that moved or was stationary with strings, halter ropes or clothesline cord about as soon as I could make a loop.

When I was about ten years old, the old country veterinarian in Lost River Valley named Bill Lambson, came to the ranch with his team and wagon to operate on a registered shorthorn bull that had ruptured himself. He watched as I practiced roping on my Dad's brown Morgan stallion, with my old raggy rope. When Bill left he gave me his new lariat rope and told me he thought I might learn to rope with a decent rope. What a difference a real lariat made! Fired me up to the extent that I hardly stopped to eat there for awhile.

**Stan Potts with Hall of Fame plaque**

About then I started breaking colts and wasn't above letting them buck and getting a little "bronc riding" practice. The neighborhood kids and I also built a bucking machine out of a 50 gallon barrel and four ropes. We all learned mighty quick how to give the hapless kid aboard that barrel a world champion ride, hauling mightily on all four ropes.

When I was about l6, I told my dad I wanted to try the local area rodeos. He pondered that for awhile and finally said, "O.K. I will pay your entry fees in whatever events you want to try for three rodeos. If you aren't making money after those three, you are on your own."

Armed with parental sanction, I went to Carey, Idaho first and got in the bareback riding, cow riding and calf roping. Didn't win any money, but Jerry Twitchell and I took his dad's race mare, "Tiny Lass" to rope on. She kindly cooperated, carrying us through the roping and giving it her all in the races as well. We put her in all the races and won enough money to make it home.

Next, Jack and Stan Swauger put on a rodeo in Patterson, Idaho for the miners and ranchers and hired us to bring our practice horses. My first rodeo money won was a second in the calf roping at that Patterson rodeo. It was a big eighteen bucks. "ON TO THE BIG TIME!"

Mackay was an Rodeo Cowboys Association (RCA) rodeo then but because there were several of us local kids trying to learn the game, they had a special amateur bareback riding contest for us. They knew it would be a crowd pleaser. I won my first buckle there.

The year I graduated from high school, 1952, Jerry Twichell and I saw a rodeo poster about the National High School Rodeo that would be held in Augusta, Montana.

We called the number and found out that because Idaho didn't have a state association we could still compete as long as we could provide them with three things. 1- They required a letter from the school principal verifying that each was a student with passing grades. 2- a publicity picture from each event we'd competed in and planned on entering; and 3- letters from three producers of rodeos in which we'd competed verifying we'd competed in at least one of their rodeos.

Jerry Twitchell, Stanley Allen from Salmon and I were the first kids from Idaho to attend a National High School Rodeo. The rodeo was the fourth National High School Rodeo with a total of possibly 70 or 80 contestants. My parents had a new Chevy pickup, we all headed to Montana, and my Dad cheered mightily from the stands.

From that time, high school rodeo has grown tremendously. The 2006 rodeo held in Springfield, Ill. had a total list of 1,563 contestants!

Stanley Allen had his dad's great little bulldogging horse, Popeye, up there. He let me ride him, which contributed greatly to my success. Popeye, a great little horse with a lot of heart, kindly cooperated with us kids to make us look good. (Popeye ended up in Gooding with Danny Gorrell who continued to make him available to us, and lots of us won on him in future years.)

At least two of the competitors at that High School Rodeo Finals, Duane Howard and Alvin Nelson, went on to be World Champion cowboys in the following years.

I ended up second in the bulldogging, third in the bareback riding and made the finals in the calf roping. I only packed one rope in the roping because the Texans were tying their calves in 10 seconds or so. I missed my loop and they both missed their first loop but they carried a second rope. Ah, a lesson learned. Poochie Appelt roped his calf in 18 seconds to win it.

The star attraction at that event for me, was the All Around Saddle. It glistened, gleamed, mesmerized, beckoned. I tied for second in the All Around with Alvin Nelson. I would have loved to win that saddle! Franklin Menke from Edgemont, South Dakota won it. But a few years earlier I would not have believed I could have done so well, with so much great competition, so felt plumb euphoric as the event wrapped up.

I had only bulldogged a very few steers up until then. Bob Robinson and his brother-in-law, Frank Anderson, had helped me with a couple at rodeos. I knew I desperately needed some kind of practice. An interesting sidelight here: I was at the rodeo in Rockland, Idaho and Bob was off in the Army in Korea. His folks invited me to stay with them. I took a big crash head first into the fence in front of the bleachers with lots of cuts on my face. Bob's dad took me up to the house and painted all the cuts with the scarlet oil wound dressing used for livestock. I was the purple faced cowboy for a couple days but the cuts all healed with no scars! I'm sure Bob got a chuckle out of that when he heard.

At the Augusta, Montana rodeo, I was still looking for that practice, being single-minded, and Oral Zumwalt, the stock contractor, had the dogging steers separated out in a small pen. He wasn't anywhere to be seen, so I decided I would just go in and catch them one at a time and practice throwing them. I learned a lot in the next few minutes. You might call it one of life's valuable lessons! Nobody had told me that they would be very protective of one another, somewhat like a mother hen protecting her chicks!

I had on a new white shirt, a new Fox hat and a pair of "Cool Dude" sun glasses when this fiasco started. I grabbed the first (and also the last), and things went rapidly down hill from there. The rest of the herd attacked me. I found out that there are lots of horns and hooves in a pen of 20 or so bulldogging steers. I'm on the bottom of the pile and can't figure out how to fight my way up out of all those t-bones, antlers, and sirloins!

When I finally did, draping my exhausted carcass over the fence with glaring cattle blowing snot in my direction and giving me the evil eye, what was left of the new white shirt was green from used grass, gray from the dirt and mud and red from someone's blood. Damn! MY blood! Worse yet, the sunglasses were history and the new Fox hat resembled an old farmer's chore hat! Certainly no longer fit for an up-and-coming RCA cowboy.

Well, Idaho joined the National High School Rodeo Association, the next year, and lots of Idaho kids have been there since 1952.

Bob Schild had watched me calf rope at a few rodeos and talked me into coming up to the University of Idaho because they needed a calf roper for their team. So I found myself enrolled at University of Idaho, but Bob ended up transferring to Colorado A and M that summer. Bob was to become the Intercollegiate champion in both Saddle Bronc and Bareback Riding.

I had pretty good luck on the team and worked all events. I won my first saddle at the Washington State Rodeo held in Kennewick, plus a couple of real gold and silver buckles. Now that's the real fuel that keeps a cowboy going!

Well, maybe I only wanted that saddle and those shiny buckles, because I only went to U of I one year and then went to ranching and rodeoing a little on weekends. It was hard to get entered in the amateur rodeos, because there were so many entrants. I went to a lot more RCA rodeos because I could get entered. I did pretty good in the bulldogging, placing at most of the rodeos I entered. Actually made more money in the bull riding. Went to eight of Harley Tucker's rodeos and got a check at every one. Yeh, ground splits, and I touched the ground early on every one!

We bought a ranch in Nevada in 1958. Harry Charters was going to sell Brandi, his great little bulldogging mare that had been Dean Oliver's first calf roping horse. I figured I'd already paid for her a couple times over in mount money but I knew she'd get me there. With Brandi's help, I was able to win the Nevada Cowboys Association Bulldogging in 1958 and 1960. I ended up second or third in the bull riding and bareback riding a couple times also and was elected president of the NCA, serving a couple of years. Around the time I was ready to quit, someone shot Brandi thru her front leg. I found her in the pasture, and sadly, had to put her down. I pretty much retired in 1961, only going to an occasional rodeo that had all-around saddles. I didn't win any.

A short 8 or 9 year career that made lots of friends. I collected a little hardware, and a few sheckles here and there. I wouldn't trade that period of my life for anything and it is a great honor to be inducted in the "Legends of Idaho Rodeo-Cowboy Hall of Fame." This happened in Gooding, Idaho on August 19, 2006.

Barbara Harp has been a great help with editing and proof reading my new book, "The Potts Factor's Return." She wryly suggests that all those ambulance rides finally paid off with this award, and noted that we just keep learning more and more about Stan Potts. Keep 'em guessing. That's always been my creed!

BARBARA, MANY THANKS FOR ALL YOUR HELP!

If you enjoyed this book, you are sure to enjoy these other two books by Stanley Potts:

**The Potts' Factor Versus Murphy's Law**

**Look Down on the Stars**

For additional copies of

**The Potts Factor's Return**

The price is $20.00 for soft cover and $25.00 for hard cover plus shipping.

You can order directly from the author:

Stanley Potts
4 Redside Way
Shoup, Idaho 83469
Website: thepottsfactor.com
Email: thepottsfactor@salmoninternet.com
(208) 394-2135